MEMORIES
OF
JOHN LENNON

HarperEntertainment
An Imprint of HarperCollins*Publishers*

MEMORIES

OF

JOHN LENNON

EDITED AND INTRODUCED BY

Yoko Ono

Frontispiece film still by Albert Maysles from *What's Happening!* © 1964 Apple Corps Ltd. Reprinted with permission. All rights reserved.

MEMORIES OF JOHN LENNON. Copyright © 2005 by Yoko Ono. All rights reserved. Printed in the United States of America. No part of this book may be used or reproduced in any manner whatsoever without written permission except in the case of brief quotations embodied in critical articles and reviews. For information address HarperCollins Publishers, 10 East 53rd Street, New York, NY 10022.

HarperCollins books may be purchased for educational, business, or sales promotional use. For information please write: Special Markets Department, HarperCollins Publishers, 10 East 53rd Street, New York, NY 10022.

FIRST EDITION

Designed by Jeffrey Pennington

Printed on acid-free paper

Library of Congress Cataloging-in-Publication Data

Memories of John Lennon / edited by Yoko Ono
   p. cm.
  ISBN-13: 978-0-06-059455-8
  ISBN-10: 0-06-059455-1
  1. Lennon, John, 1940–1980. 2. Rock musicians—Biography. I. Ono, Yoko.

ML420.L38M46 2005
782.42166'092—dc22
  [B]   2005046275

05 06 07 08 09 ❖/RRD 10 9 8 7 6 5 4 3 2 1

This book is a present from me to John who, after the breakup of the Beatles, did not know that he still had so many sweet and genuine friends who thought well of him. Happy birthday, John. We are all thankful that you were here with us.

Big kiss, yoko

CONTENTS

CONTENTS

My Memory of John

When John passed away so suddenly that night, I felt as though half of me flew away with him. My body, especially my knees, shook so badly, I had to hold on to a friend to walk out of the hospital. Spring came and went. Summer. I was surprised that the leaves were shining so intensely when John was no more. It seemed like a crime, that everything else was still so alive. Fall was beautiful. And Winter. I realized then that the winters would be hard for some time.

Twenty-five years have passed since then. I am all right when I am with people, my son, and my daughter. I smile, I laugh. I look up at the sky and let my heart dance. I hug my children—even though it's more accurate to say that they hug me, since they are much larger than me now. But when I'm alone, when the evening light starts to drench the world in pink, in the dark of the night and at dawn, my heart still shakes and will not stop.

People always ask me when will I write about my life with John. I repeat my answer that I am not ready yet. Will I ever be ready? I don't feel I would be. I feel I could not open that part of my heart while it's still shaking.

This book was such a blessing for me. I cherished reading each one of the vignettes. Each writer was so sincere in their love for John, it immediately relaxed me. They were so funny, too. Great wits! Fantastic minds! I could not believe that so many of John's and my friends suddenly revealed themselves as great writers. I kept saying to them in my mind, "Don't stop. You should have been a writer. Well, you still could be." They made me laugh belly laughs. I haven't laughed so much since Woody Allen's last film, I thought. And that was quite a while ago. . . . I laughed and laughed. And then I cried. Tears were streaming out of me, uncontrollably, and would not stop even after the last page—which came too soon. . . .

What a beautiful project this book turned out to be. I hope you'll enjoy it as much as I have. As John used to say after our successful projects—in our eyes, that is—we have to make a "son of" very soon. Thank you, my friends, for still carrying those memories and sharing them with us, and especially, with me. I am a lucky woman.

YOKO ONO LENNON
Spring 2005

JANE ALEXANDER

WHEN I FIRST HEARD "IMAGINE," AND THE SOFT, GENTLE VOICE OF JOHN SINGING, I WAS QUITE OVERWHELMED. THE SONG SEEMED TO ENCAPSULATE ALL WE IN THE 1960S DREAMED OF: A WORLD WITH NO VIOLENCE, NO RACISM, NO war, no assassinations—a world possible through envisioning it to be so. I still believe it, and every time I hear the song, it enforces my belief. We can have peace, harmony, beauty and love if we make that our constant vision for the future, if we imagine it and live it ourselves every day. That was John's gift to us, all through his remarkable song.

Jane Alexander, a veteran of stage and screen, received a 1969 Tony Award for her work in *The Great White Hope*. She has appeared in numerous feature films, including *All the President's Men* and *Kramer vs. Kramer*.

Lennonism   TARIQ ALI

OUR FIRST DIRECT CONTACT IN 1969 WAS FORMAL. I
WAS EDITING THE *BLACK DWARF*, A RADICAL POLITICO-
CULTURAL MAGAZINE. WE HAD PUBLISHED "AN OPEN
LETTER TO JOHN LENNON"—A SAVAGE REVIEW OF THE
Beatles' album *Revolution* by John Hoyland, our music/popular cul-
ture critic. John Lennon had been busted by the cops. The *Black
Dwarf* used the occasion to discuss the lyrics of the *Revolution* album
seriously. Hoyland wrote:

> *Above all: perhaps now you'll see what it is you're (we're)
> up against. Not nasty people, not even neurosis or spiri-
> tual undernourishment. What we're confronted with is a
> repressive, vicious, authoritarian system. A system which
> is inhuman and immoral, because it deprives 99 percent
> of humanity of the right to live their lives their own way.
> A system which will screw you if you step out of line and
> behave just a tiny bit differently from the way those in
> power want.*
>
> *Such a system—such a society—is so racked by con-
> tradiction and tension and unhappiness that all relation-*

ships within it are poisoned. You know this. You know, from your own experience, how little control over their lives working-class people are permitted to have. . . . How can love and kindness between human-beings grow in such a society? It can't. Don't you see that now? The system has got to be changed before people can live the full, loving lives that you have said you want.

Now do you see what was wrong with your record Revolution*? That record was no more revolutionary than* Mrs. Dale's Diary*. In order to change the world we've got to understand what's wrong with the world. And then, destroy it. Ruthlessly. . . . There is no such thing as a polite revolution.*

The tone of the letter was undoubtedly patronizing, and we thought he would ignore it. But a week later he sent a reply to John Hoyland with a covering note hoping I would publish it. We did:

Who do you think you are? What do you think you know? I'm not only up against the establishment but you, too, it seems. I know what I'm up against—narrow minds—rich/poor. All your relationships may be poisoned—it depends how you look at it. What kind of system do you propose and who would run it?

I don't remember saying Revolution *was revolutionary—fuck* Mrs. Dale*. Listen to all three versions (*Revolution *1, 2 and 9) then try again, dear John. . . .*

You're obviously on a destruction kick. I'll tell you what's wrong with the world—people, so do you want to destroy them? Ruthlessly? Until we change your/our heads—there's no chance. Tell me of one successful revolution. Who fucked up Communism . . . ? Sick Heads and nothing else. Do you think all the enemy wear capitalist badges so that you can shoot them? It's a bit naïve, John. You seem to think it's just a class war. . . .

Look man, I was/am not against you. Instead of splitting hairs about the Beatles and the Stones—think a little bigger—look at the world we're living in and ask yourself: why? And then—come and join us.

Love,
John Lennon

PS—You smash it—I'll build around it.

As these extracts suggest, it was a spirited exchange.

After that there was a long silence. And, as was also common in those days, there was soon a split in the *Black Dwarf*. How strange it seems now and how stupid and destructive, but that's the way we were. The Leninists left to set up *Red Mole* and moved from swinging Soho to proletarian Pentonville Road, a seedy zone near Kings Cross station in London.

One day John rang and we talked. He suggested a meeting and a week later he and Yoko showed up at my bed-sit in North London with a delicious Japanese take-away as supper. We discussed the state of the world, including the state of the student movement in Japan. John's views had sharpened considerably since the letters in the *Black Dwarf*. He told me that, like Mick Jagger, he had wanted to march on the big anti-Vietnam war demos but the Beatles' manager, Brian Epstein, had forbidden any such outing. Epstein was fearful that the group might be denied visas to the States, which would be a commercial disaster. John always regretted having obeyed his manager, but that was in the past. The biggest and best influence in his life was now Yoko Ono. I was in no doubt that Yoko had radicalized him further on the artistic and the political front. She had also been accused of breaking up the Beatles and we laughed a great deal at the suggestion. He was angered by the racist gibes against Yoko in the tabloid press. I suggested they should be taken as compliments. It would be awful if the creeps who attacked her decided to turn their coats. Before they left, I suggested an interview with both of them and he agreed, wondering aloud whether it would be appropriate since "*Red Mole* was very serious and interviewing me might lower the tone." He wasn't joking, but I assured him that an interview would be enormously helpful for our little newspaper. I asked if I could bring my colleague Robin Blackburn—more attuned to popular culture than myself—to which he readily agreed.

A week later, a large limo pulled up outside our offices to the astonishment of bystanders. Robin and I piled in and were driven to Tittenhurst. We spoke for most of the day, saw one of Yoko's avant-garde films (which Robin Blackburn simply adored) and were driven back to London. The interview had gone extremely well. Both John and Yoko had been disarmingly frank. All that was now left was the editing.

The very next morning John rang. He had been so inspired by our interview that he had written a new song. Could he sing it on the phone? He could. That was how I first heard "Power to the People."

We met several times after that, sometimes before a recording session at the Abbey Road Studios, more often at Tittenhurst. Robin and I took a French friend, Régis Debray, to one of these sessions. I first heard the words of "Imagine" at the kitchen table in Tittenhurst.

"The Politburo approves, John," I joked at the time, wondering whether I would have been in a minority on the Politburo on this question. His lyrics had moved beyond matrimonial moonings. Love and happiness now became a feminist call for a new way of life. Here again, Yoko's influence was visible. The fantastic, as well as the surreal, were given a rest. Lennon, as Epstein feared, had become ultrasubversive and political. "Working Class Hero" and "The Luck of the Irish" did not please the conservative critics, but were enormously popular.

It was on one of these visits to Tittenhurst that he told me how fed up they were with England. It was too parochial and racist, Yoko hated it and so did he and they were moving to New York. I could understand all this, but did warn him that there were too many kooks in that country and he should be careful. During his first year in New York we spoke on the phone, but soon lost touch. Computers, alas, had not yet been invented.

Together with the rest of the world, one felt a great deal of pain the day he died. I think the tribute he would have loved was the spontaneous grief in Moscow as kids rushed to the Lenin Hills and sang "Back in the U.S.S.R." I thought of him during the giant global demonstrations against the Bush-Blair war on Iraq. His spirit was marching with us.

Tariq Ali is a noted journalist, historian and activist. He interviewed John Lennon and Yoko Ono for his underground magazine *Red Mole* in 1971.

TERRI AUGELLO

Not long ago, my daughter, Alicia, staged a benefit for African children stricken with AIDS, and she thrilled us all by bringing onto the stage Babyface, who sat atop a simple stool and dueted on his acoustic guitar with Alicia on her piano, singing "Imagine." The clarity, beauty and magnificence of that John Lennon tune both moved me and transformed me back in time for a moment. I can clearly remember in 1964, at age thirteen, getting ready for school as my clock radio blared out a new tune from the "mopheads" from England called "I Want to Hold Your Hand." I wasn't that impressed at first, but as I grew up and as the Beatles' popularity and record catalogue grew, so did my admiration and love for John Lennon and the Beatles. I wore my albums thin, playing them on my dad's hi-fi stereo, listening to all those songs I felt were written just for me and screamed with all the other girls when John and the Beatles appeared on the *Ed Sullivan Show.* It seemed like we all grew up together, defying the norm, and when all was said and done, John's music defined my generation. I remember sitting in my New York apartment, a young mother-to-be, glued to the TV news, stunned at the footage of John's assassination that had taken place only a few blocks away in front of the Dakota, and chills went down my spine. How could we have lost such a gifted man? How could we survive that loss, musically or politically? Flash forward some twenty-plus years later, as I refocused on the stage, and there was my baby girl, sending John's musical masterpiece into the air, the perfect song to highlight the plight of the AIDS pandemic, and I thought, yes, John would approve. For surely, his memory and talent lives on. Influencing still the talent of all the generations to come, and protesting from the grave, the issues that can only be properly highlighted by the music and attitude John seemed to stand for. Now that's a tribute no one can deny.

Terri Augello is the mother and biggest influence of Grammy Award–winning singer/songwriter Alicia Keys. She raised Alicia as a single mom while working as a paralegal and actress in New York City.

JOAN BAEZ

Joan Baez is a folk musician and activist whose many honors include the Earl Warren Award for commitment to human and civil rights issues.

Aug 21 2004

Dear Yoko,

This drawing was done upside down with my left hand. What I think it portrays is John as a member of the four, which is the only time I ever spent any time with him. Everything surrounding them was completely insane. They had discovered that the Coke machine in their sitting room in the hotel was free. They were thrilled! I made them tea and they were amazed that I knew to heat the tea pot before making tea. Hundreds of girls were screeching on the street below.

John as I remember him was both bright and enormously funny.

I hope you can use the drawing, and best of luck with this project. I look forward to seeing the finished product.

Sincerely,
Joan Baez

Harry Benson

To me the most important car ride John Lennon and the Beatles ever made was from the Plaza Hotel on their way to their first appearance on the *Ed Sullivan Show* in New York City on February 9, 1964.

It started at breakfast time. My room was just down the hall, and I was having breakfast with the four of them in their suite at the Plaza. No one seemed to be eating much. Everything was relatively calm. They were all talking about the *Ed Sullivan Show* and what they were going to sing and John said something about just going with the most popular songs.

Outside in the street there was chaos. Police were wrestling with little girls who were climbing up back stairways or passing themselves off as hotel guests. A few got up but were stopped outside the room.

Back in my room about 1:30 PM with cameras ready—I always keep my cameras ready on a news story and this was a big news story. I was on the bed as I thought they were going to the theater a bit later. There was a bang on my door. John came in and said they were going now and for me to come with them and stay as close as I could or the police would cut me off. Right enough, there was pandemonium trying to get to the car. Downstairs, a policeman tried to stop me from getting into their limo and to his credit John said, "If Harry doesn't go, I don't go."

Paul, George, Ringo and I got in first and John followed. They were too close for me to take their photo inside the limo (it was not a stretch limo like we have today). They all leaned over and put their heads down so I could get a picture of the fans chasing after us as we drove off. John and I were on the jump seats and in the front were the driver and Mal Evans. It all happened in a matter of seconds. While I was taking the picture from inside the car, John held my camera bag because we were so crammed into such a small space.

Photograph © Harry Benson 1964.

When we got to the CBS studio, it was the same chaos again. I jumped out first and John kept me next to him because the studio door opened and slammed shut like an elastic band.

I sat around with John drinking Coca-Colas waiting for the show to start. We never went back to the hotel after the rehearsal—it would have been too hectic. And when they went on live television, as everyone knows, they were sensational.

Back in the hotel we had dinner in their suite. It was very quiet as they had turned off the phone in the room. They all seemed relieved that it had gone so well.

After George, Paul and Ringo went to bed, John and I stayed up drinking whiskey and talking for another hour, talking basically about nothing—our childhood and things like that. John said he had been to Glasgow, where I am from, and had seen the same faces he saw in Liverpool. I asked him if he would ever go back and live in Liverpool and he said no. John talked a bit about America and said he found the American press easier than the British press. Still wearing his tie, he had taken off his jacket and shoes. They all complained that the shoes were uncomfortable. The telephone messages, which had been held at the front desk, were sent up and John sat reading them. The congratulations had come in from everywhere and everyone—from senators who wanted to bring their children to meet the Beatles to other artists saying they were a smash.

As the next day would be busy with so many people wanting interviews, I said good night and went to my room. It had been an historic day.

Years later, I met Yoko Ono. I had heard a lot of stories about her, but after meeting her it was quite easy to see why John had loved her. Intelligent, funny, perceptive, with good manners, I think she was the mirror image of John's best qualities. Although I never photographed John after 1966, I miss him.

Harry Benson is a photographer who has documented famous faces from Muhammad Ali to Elizabeth Taylor in fifty years as a photojournalist. In 1964 he accompanied the Beatles on their first U.S. tour.

CHUCK BERRY

SINCE THE TIME THEY HAD ONE OF THEIR FIRST HITS WITH "ROLL OVER BEETHOVEN," I'VE ALWAYS FELT VERY CLOSE TO THE BEATLES. I FEEL AS IF I LOST A LITTLE PART OF MYSELF WHEN JOHN DIED.

Chuck Berry is one of rock and roll music's founding fathers and a 1986 inductee into the Rock and Roll Hall of Fame. His compositions include "Johnny B. Goode" and "Back in the U.S.A."

The Beatles

Eric's drawing for Grandma and Gra

Eric's drawing for Grandma and Grandpa.

JELLO BIAFRA

ONCE UPON A TIME, I WAS LYING IN BED IN THE DARK WHEN A FLYING SAUCER BOLTED OUT OF THE RADIO AND ZAPPED ME RIGHT BETWEEN THE EYES! THE MUSIC WAS ROCK 'N' ROLL, IT WAS 1965 AND BEATLEMANIA WAS IN full swing. I was seven years old.

My Dad had been fiddling with the dial, desperate to find something—anything—that would make me go to sleep. One clang of the electric guitar and I was hooked—"Leave it here! Leave it here!"

Within days I knew I'd found a special new friend, and my life would never be the same again. I knew what I wanted to be when I grew up. Deep down I never really wanted to do anything else. While my parents thought I was asleep, I'd be jumping up and down on my bed, pretending I was the song on the radio—air singer, air guitar, air organ. In my secret world, I was pretty cool.

From day one I went straight for the hard stuff, the wilder the song, the more I liked it. Faves included early Stones, Paul Revere and the Raiders, Animals, Music Machine, and "Denver's own" Moonrakers (remember when AM radio played local bands?). The Animals' singer was named Eric, just like me.

And day in, day out there was the Beatles. They weren't quite one of my super-favorites, but they were the group everyone outside my secret radio world knew. So they were my identity.

I drew mop-haired stick figures with my crayons in class. They were always on the radio, several songs a night. "Day Tripper" squeaked the bedsprings with the best of 'em. My goateed, neobeatnik pottery teacher nicknamed me "the Beatle" after I stacked clods of clay in the form of the Fab Four, and eventually got Ringo's drum to stand up.

I remember clear as day the excitement when I saw the Beatles on TV on *Hullabaloo.* By then they were lunch boxes, thermoses, a board game, even a cartoon show. I liked them better in human form when my dad took me to see *A Hard Day's Night.* What a life! I've had dreams of those chase scenes ever since.

A girl named Erika in my second grade class also knew about the Beatles. She'd giggle at the thought of listening to rock and roll on the radio. It was so deliciously naughty. One day the teacher announced, "Mrs. Demmon [the office lady's] son is coming to show us his dog." Erika and I looked at each other, eyes wide. We knew that could only mean one thing—Bob Demmon, the leader of Colorado's main band, the Astronauts, is coming to our class—and we're the only ones who know who he is!

The big day came, and a soft-spoken Bob Demmon showed up with his Alaskan Malamute. He mostly stared at the floor and mumbled, as the dog silently tiptoed between rows and let us pet him. "He doesn't say much," and neither did Bob. I guess he was really nervous; this wasn't screaming teenage girls, this was a classroom full of little kids! Horror! Gasp! His white sweater was kind of hip, but his hair wasn't nearly as cool as the Beatles. Thus ended my first encounter with a rock star.

Then the really big day came—the Beatles were coming to Denver! Excitement was in the air, or at least on the air. But, of course, I didn't get to go—too young. I understood, but I still haven't forgiven my parents for not taking me to see the Monkees a year later. The opening act was Jimi Hendrix.

The Beatles must really like Colorado, thought I. It's been weeks and weeks since they played Bears Stadium and they're still coming down to play on the radio. . . . Dad finally broke down and told me the news, "No, that's not the Beatles in the room, or Paul Revere either. They play records on the radio." First no Santa Claus, now this! I've never quite trusted pop culture or corporate media again.

I'd get tired of the radio and leave it off for a while, go back a few months or a year later, then leave it off again. I came back to stay with a vengeance around age ten. Rock was heavier and so were the times. Steppenwolf ruled, so did the Who, and Three Dog Night, of all people (c'mon, I was ten!). I really dug who I thought was a black soul singer named Creedence Clearwater. Then it was on to Led Zeppelin, to Black Sabbath, to Alice Cooper, the Stooges, MC5, Pink Fairies and beyond.

By now my relationship with the Beatles had changed. You couldn't get away from them. "Everyone likes the Beatles" . . . "Everyone likes the Beatles" . . . Every third song on the air was the Beatles. The most straight-laced squares at my school liked the Beatles. Every purple bubble gum chickie liked the Beatles. I tried to turn them on to my "superior taste" and record collector knowledge by DJ-ing at my high school during lunch hour, but all they wanted to hear was the fucking Beatles. "Haven't you heard *Abbey Road* enough times already? Can't wait three or four hours 'til you get home? Doesn't anyone wanna hear something new??? Anyone???"

"No, play the Beatles. Everyone likes the Beatles."

They were the omnipresent everywhere, the ultimate pop narcotic, even more so than baseball. "Everyone likes the Beatles."

Even my Jerry Vale–addled grandmother liked the Beatles. Her radio station and my parents' station played constant Beatles, too. I dug "Get Back" and loved "Back in the U.S.S.R." and Plastic Ono's "Cold Turkey," but felt downright rebellious toward the phenomenon known as the Beatles. You couldn't get away from them, still can't. I'd heard so many of their songs so many times I didn't care if I heard them again.

Or so I thought, as I left home for San Francisco and dove straight into punk rock. Whaddya know, more Beatles. A leather-clad John Lennon from his rockabilly days hung next to more than a few Pistols and Clash posters at parties. For a while I lived with Dead Kennedys' bassist Klaus Flouride in the house that inspired our song, "Let's Lynch the Landlord." Every day when he came home from his temp job, Klaus would open his bedroom window, kneel at the sill and listen to *Abbey Road* with his head sandwiched between the speakers, staring out the window like a shell-shocked mental patient. I thought, "Hey, dude, we're in a punk band, one of the few that still scares people. . . . Why are you doing this? What are you hiding from? What's so great about the Beatles, anyway? . . ."

Darkness fell toward the end of 1980. Soon Reagan would take office. We had no idea what we were in for. I was sitting at the counter at a long-gone North Beach Italian restaurant called Luigi's. New Wave scribe and future major label mogul Howie Klein sat down beside me. "Did you hear about John Lennon? Shot on the street in New York. Did you hear about Darby Crash? O.D.'d. Committed suicide."

Wham. . . . At first I was more upset about Darby because I knew him. Darby Crash, the snarling ringmaster of the Germs, hands down one of the most insane bands in history. Everyone at the punk show around the corner at Mabuhay Gardens was upset about Darby, even people who didn't like him or the Germs. Fights broke out among my friends.

The morning after it began to sink in . . . someone shot John Lennon. . . . Some fucked-up narcissistic Christian bigot shot John Lennon. I remember Bowie glibly predicting some day a rock star would be assassinated, but why John Lennon? Why? Of all people, why would anyone want to shoot John Lennon?!

Only then did it truly dawn on me how important John Lennon has been to music, world evolution and my own life. When the Beatles grew their hair, we grew our hair. As theirs got longer (especially John's) so did ours. Hair was no longer fashion—it was rebellion. When they turned on and went psychedelic, so did we. When they made the rock album more important than the single, so did everyone else. And when they made it okay for someone besides folk singers to take a stand on important issues, how could any artist in any field not show where they stood?

They could have been the Fab Four forever, in the same haircuts and the same suits playing the same songs over and over again to stadiums packed with sheeplike oldies fans. They had the spirit and class to use their power to go so much further and do so much more. Finally, the yin and yang of Lennon/McCartney penetrated my thick skull. The swashbuckling admiral was obviously John.

It was John who made Nixon's enemies list, singing "All You Need Is Love" during a bloody, illegal war. It was John who quietly helped the yippies in small but important ways like lending them his postage meter. Most important, it was John more than anyone who opened the gate for the Beatles and all popular music to sweep way beyond the confines of "silly love songs" and blossom into the cultural force that remade our world and stopped the Vietnam War. When John sang, people listened. Revolution? All right . . . violence? Mao? No. Let's keep our heads. And it was John who was unafraid to use his visibility and star power as a voice for peace, in the actions outside of music with Yoko. A few laughed; many more were lifted and energized.

The shock, memorials and remembrances poured in after John died—on the news, in the papers and in our bedrooms by the record player. I realized how much I love John Lennon and how much I have loved him for a very long time. I especially loved the *Playboy* interview that came out right after he was gone. John, the human being spitting wisdom, comfortable with his own intelligence, talent and place in the world. Sure, he was caustic at times, but in just the way I like. Here was a beloved mainstream pop figure dishing out the same inspiring brain food I'd expect from a really good interview with Frank Zappa or Iggy Pop or any number of important punk pioneers. He was warm, he was funny and obviously someone who still gave a shit. Here was what the mainstream was missing—a conscience. He seemed like he'd be wonderful to talk to. He felt like my friend.

Ever notice sometimes that a song you didn't like much as a kid now brings tears to your eyes? For me, one of those is "Imagine." After John died it became so touching and so sweet it is almost painful to listen to.

> *Imagine all the people . . .*
> *Sharing all the world . . .*
> *Living life in peace . . .*

Imagine . . .
If John had lived.
Imagine . . . If John had lived.
Hard to say if we ever would have met or hit it off, or what he would have thought of punk music, especially mine.

But imagine—what would he have said about the Reagan era, and what we let ourselves turn into? What would he have said about Tipper Gore and her Right-Wing Christian pals' antimusic crusade? So many major voices were silent.

Where was Bruce Springsteen? Where was Bob Dylan? Where was John Lennon???? Somehow, I can't imagine him staying quiet.

What would he have to say about the Bush-era Dark Ages?

Would "Revolution" have been sold into a Nike TV commercial?

Recently we lost Johnny Cash. Many of my friends and I were puzzled—why are we so upset about this? We knew it was coming. He lived a great life. Why does this hurt so bad? A voice piped up in the car riding through L.A. one night, "He was our Abe Lincoln."

Yeah. . . .

I can't even imagine what that makes John Lennon.

Wherever you are, John, your spirit lives—and in all the right ways. By now I hope Wesley Willis has given you a friendly head butt.

Jello Biafra is the former lead singer of seminal punk rock group the Dead Kennedys. He continues to record both music and spoken word pieces on his own Alternative Tentacles record label.

CILLA BLACK

IT WAS THANKS TO JOHN LENNON THAT I GOT MY BIG BREAK IN MUSIC. I FIRST MET JOHN WHEN I WAS FIFTEEN YEARS OLD AND ATTENDING THE ANFIELD COMMERCIAL COLLEGE. MY GIRLFRIEND PAULINE SAID TO ME THAT YOU REALLY ought to come down and see my boyfriend play at the Iron Door, which was a sort of glorified youth club there at Anfield. Well, her boyfriend was George Harrison and the band was the Beatles. We went in a crowd of girls from the school, and they all said to the boys onstage, "Give Cilla a go!" because I had been singing at lunch parties and clubs in Liverpool, wherever I could, so they said, "Let her have a go!" and from the stage John said "Okay, Cyrill"—he called me "Cyrill," the man's name, he was always calling me that, his little joke because of course he knew my real name—John said, "Okay Cyrill, show us what you've got!" So I got up and sang a version of [Gershwin's] "Summertime," the *Porgy & Bess* number.

Some time afterward I was at the Majestic Ballroom in Birkenhead, and Brian Epstein came up to me and said, "I've never heard you sing, I want you to sing with the boys tonight." So I sang "Summertime" again, with the Beatles playing behind me, but I was terribly, terribly nervous, and Brian was not at all impressed, and

I thought, well okay, that's that, I'll just be singing around the clubs in Liverpool.

A few months later I was singing in a club called the Blue Angel and after I finished my set Brian came up to me and said, "Why didn't you sing like that at the Majestic Ballroom?" I had no idea he was even in the club that night, but he loved what he heard and asked to manage me right then. I later asked Ringo if he had asked Brian to give me another listen, because Ringo and I were friends, but he just looked at me and said, "It wasn't me, it was John." I thank him to this day, because but for John, Brian never would have given me a second shot after that awful first audition. It truly changed my life.

He did stuff like that, which you'd think was totally out of character for him, because he liked to put on this angry young man front, you know, a man's man, aloof, but behind that was a very warmhearted guy, and really quite shy, and with an acid sense of humor. I remember I did a big TV special, called "Around the Beatles." I sang a song John and Paul had given me, "Love of the Loved," while standing at the top of a flight of steps and wearing a very short miniskirt. Sitting at the bottom of the steps were the Beatles, and afterward, during the applause, John whispered mischievously in my ear, "I could see tomorrow's washing," meaning he could see my underthings, of course, and normally I'd have been mortified, but there I was on TV, so I just laughed. He was always trying to throw you like that.

Cilla Black is a singer and television personality who, like her friends the Beatles, rose to stardom from the clubs of Liverpool under the auspices of Brian Epstein and George Martin. She achieved twenty consecutive British top forty records in the early 1960s before moving to television to host a series of successful programs on the BBC.

BONO

"oh my lord/love for the first
time in my life ... I could see"
Bono age 12

Bono is the lead singer of rock band U2, a 2005 inductee into the Rock and Roll Hall of Fame.
The Dublin-born musician is also a noted human rights activist.

JAMES BROWN

THE BEATLES WERE ONE-OF-A-KIND AND A BLESSING TO THE MUSIC WORLD, EACH AND EVERY ONE OF THEM. JOHN WAS EXTREMELY TALENTED — HE SEEMED TO HAVE A LOT ON HIS MIND, BUT IT NEVER HURT HIS MUSIC, SO I CAN TRULY say: I think there will never be another like that beautiful brother, may God bless his soul and his family. John, we will never forget you.

James Brown has earned the nicknames "The Godfather of Soul" and "The Hardest-Working Man in Show Business" for his legendary songwriting and stage performances.

PETER BROWN

THE MEMORIES I LOVE TO RECALL ABOUT JOHN LENNON ARE THOSE OF PRIVATE MOMENTS WE SHARED; THEY SO WELL CAPTURED WHAT A COMPLEX, REMARKABLE AND CON-TRADICTORY MAN HE WAS. JOHN, OF COURSE TO MANY people, could be terrifying. He had a quick wit and an acid tongue, which frequently came over as nasty, ruthless and rude, an image he rather enjoyed having. He was impatient with people who couldn't keep up with him, and his stare—especially when he wore glasses—looked cold and forbidding.

John's tough side was built up as a young man. Abandoned by his father, orphaned by the death of his mother and brought up by a tough, strict aunt, John's pain and alienation fueled a creative mind in art school, the angry Teddy Boy and later the tough in the leather jacket who found solace in American rhythm and blues and rock and roll.

There is no doubt that within this complex person there was also a very sensitive being. I saw this over the years.

I think that the close bond that existed between Brian Epstein and John was largely as a result of them sharing and seeing in each other complicated personalities which were often unhappy and frequently frustrated; they, as perhaps no others, understood each other. John always regarded the Beatles as his band and there is no question that when Brian offered management to the band John was supportive because he believed he could forge a bond with Brian. He was always the closest Beatle to Brian.

I think my good relationship with John was as a result of my being Brian's closest friend. John understood how Brian and I tried to help and support each other emotionally over the years.

There were many quiet occasions when I saw John's kind and gentle side. The one I will always remember best was after I came back from Brian Epstein's funeral. The funeral was held secretly and the Beatles were asked not to attend out of concern that it would turn into a press orgy.

On my return, I met with just the four Beatles, Neil Aspinall and Mal Evans. As I walked into the room, everyone asked me how the funeral went and a discussion started about what we were going to do now without Brian. After a few minutes John came to me and put his arms around me and asked in the gentlest of voices if I was all right. He knew that the two people most emotionally affected by Brian's death were him and me, and only he understood how totally devastated I was by Brian's death because he felt the same way, too.

Peter Brown managed business affairs for the Beatles after the 1967 death of Brian Epstein. He also served as best man at the wedding of John Lennon and Yoko Ono in 1969.

MIKE CADWALLADER

I'M ONE OF SEVEN COUSINS OF JOHN'S GENERATION, WE ARE ALL THE CHILDREN OF WHAT I THINK EVEN JOHN DESCRIBED AS THE "FAMOUS FIVE SISTERS"—WHO WERE HIS MOTHER, JULIA; HARRIET; MY MOTHER, ANNE; ELIZABETH; and Mary, who was commonly known as Mimi. The whole family really, and all us cousins, revolved around these five sisters, kind of benign dictators in a way, who ensured we all behaved. In our younger days I suppose we were all given this regime, we were all fairly conventional, except for John. In some way there was always something about him that marked him out as a little different, and we certainly—the younger cousins, John was the third eldest of the seven—the younger four always sort of looked up to him in awe. I don't know why, we just did, and that must tell you something about him.

When I was growing up I'd get together with my cousin David. We'd spend most of our weekends at Aunt Mimi's home, Mendips, and we would see John there when he wasn't spending the weekend down at his mother's, which he did often. That wasn't at all strange for any of us. People ask, well how was it with John living with his auntie and his mother living down the road? But the whole family was kind of an entity, and during holidays we all used to decamp and spend it in Edinburgh. It was all a very close and family-oriented time back in the 1950s. John was very close to Uncle George, Mimi's husband. An interesting gentleman, George was the man of the house when John was there. Uncle George was sort of a working man, he had been part owner of a dairy with his brother, and he'd been doing other jobs later on. He had a degree of sophistication and learning, and he could talk about things, he had some language

skills, and having been in the army he'd seen a bit of the world and other cultures. I think that fascinated John and created a close intellectual bond between the two of them. Uncle George, in his way, helped a lot in forming John's character and outlook.

John and his mother is something else entirely. She was absolutely incredible, an absolute star, so unusually avant-garde for her time, and indeed for our family. While the other four sisters were rather more sedate, Julia was a tremendous personality—there was always fun when she was around. She was either laughing or being outrageous, which in a way I think that came through to John. That's the side of him that his mother gave him, a sort of outgoing, performance type of personality.

During our holidays, when we weren't just circulating all around the houses in Liverpool, we spent time up in Edinburgh. Certainly, we would all wind up as a gang on sev-

John, age eleven, and Mike, age four, circa 1951.

eral occasions, usually over the Easter holidays. I can confirm the oft-quoted story about John playing his harmonica on the coach, entertaining all the travelers. I remember chugging along on this coach with John on his harmonica playing "I Love to Go A-Wandering" and all these other songs, not pop music, but traveler's songs that kept everyone happy during the journey.

Holidays in Edinburgh were fairly normal, though the funniest thing was when John came up on a holiday to the north of Scotland, where Mater's—we called Aunt Elizabeth "Mater"—husband's family home was located. David and I used to go up there regularly during the summer, helping Uncle Bert with doing repairs and maintenance to the house and outbuildings and cutting hay and digging potatoes—anything he gave us to do. We did that for three weeks of our four-week holiday, and on the fourth week he gave us some time off to go fishing or to the beach. On one occasion, John joined in this trip, and he *hated* it, because the man was not put on Earth to do manual work—a mark of his being an artist, I guess—and being asked to fetch and carry and dig and cut and cement and paint and do brickwork for three weeks was just not his cup of tea at all. He didn't do hammering nails or mending fences or anything, and to be asked to do it for three weeks was just absolute hell on earth for him. It was quite funny, really, he had to join in but not with any enthusiasm or dedication—I think it was a nightmare for the poor lad.

The good side about it though, was that most evenings we used to go up a hill just behind the house to visit a friend of the family, and they had a wind-up gramophone. John quite enjoyed that, even though the music was mainly Jimmy Shand and his band, a Scottish group playing traditional Scottish music. Still, it was music.

As we got toward the end of the 1950s, David and I were still at Mendips every weekend. At that time, John had started hitting it with the Beatles, so we tended not to see him until about four o'clock in the afternoon, when he'd come down and we'd watch a bit of television—I think *Oh Boy!* was one of the programs and *Six-Five Special* was the other. So, we'd watch those with him, and then he'd be getting ready to go out and Neil [Aspinall] would call around for him in the van, and that would be it, he'd be off.

I didn't see John play very much. I was at the fete at St. Peter's Church with the rest of the family to see him with the Quarry Men. I also went to a couple sessions at the Cavern, when they played there, but not so much around the clubs in Liverpool. It was a little bit hairy in those days—one didn't go out by one's self. As time went on, the Beatles started becoming famous. One of the last occasions I saw him was when the *Please Please Me* album came out. He was still living at Mendips at the time and he came dashing in with copies of the record. It was all extremely exciting to see this going on, he was absolutely over the moon, couldn't believe it—"We've made an album, we've made an LP!" He was absolutely beside himself, it was just so exciting, things like that just didn't happen, nobody had seen anything like it before.

There was always just that "something" about John. We lived in a pretty conventional, postwar, 1950s family, and he had a sort of aura, a feeling. He had no idea of what he was going to do. He certainly wasn't going to get a job—that's what people did in the 1950s, you left school and you got a job. But there was no way he was going to get one, so what the hell was he going to do?

Those two books were published, *In His Own Write* and *A Spaniard in the Works*. That was always his great passion, writing his ditties and his school magazine and the like. There was something going on there which, one way or another, was going to come to the fore and by sheer chance, the timing and the way of the world at the time, everything just clicked. He was just one of those people— you knew when he was in the room—heads turned without anything having to be said or done, you just knew he was there, and something had changed about the day, or the place you were at. Indefinable, really.

Mike Cadwallader is John Lennon's cousin and grew up with him in Liverpool.

RAY CHARLES

I MET THE BEATLES AROUND 1962, WHEN I WAS TOURING GERMANY; THOSE BOYS WERE MY INTERMISSION BAND IN HAMBURG AND STUTTGART. THEY'D HURRY IN DURING INTERMISSION AND PLAY A FEW SONGS TO KEEP THINGS warmed up. There was no way of knowing that in a year they were gonna change the world, but they sounded good and were nice guys. Backstage afterward, we would sit and bullshit and say we loved each other's music—the typical thing that people in our musical brotherhood all do. See, we were just common people, working together.

As for John Lennon, I was spellbound and hurt and upset when he died, because he was a brilliant musician, and I respected what the man stood for. John Lennon was one of our own, and losing him just makes me mad as shit. We've got to have some damned gun-control laws, and psychiatrists should examine the people who buy them. Hell, anything that can kill people should be controlled; it's easier to get a gun in this country than a driver's license.

I loved the Beatles' music enough to record it, and I scrutinize something *very* carefully before I do. Each song was a beauty; "The Long and Winding Road" made me cry the first time I heard it. People ask me, "Ray, what's your favorite Beatles song? How do you compare 'Yesterday' and 'Eleanor Rigby' to 'Georgia' and 'What'd I Say'?" Hell, that's like asking, "Which tastes better, red beans or cabbage?" Don't you know, they *all* taste good. Yes, I'm gonna miss that man and his wonderful talent.

Ray Charles was a versatile singer, songwriter and pianist whose unique talents defied category. He received numerous honors including several lifetime achievement awards, and was inducted into the Rock and Roll Hall of Fame in 1986. He died in 2004 at the age of seventy-three.

JACKIE DeSHANNON

I HAD THE EXTRAORDINARY PRIVILEGE OF MEETING JOHN LENNON IN 1964. I HAD BEEN INVITED TO BE AN OPENING ACT FOR THE BEATLES' FIRST EXTENSIVE TOUR OF THE UNITED STATES. I REMEMBER FEELING A CONNECTION with John even before we met, knowing we both attended art college. Flying from city to city on their private plane provided us lots of time to get to know one another.

John was truly the lightness of being. What impressed me the most was his humility. Just the guy next door. I loved his wicked sense of humor. We played jokes on each other and had countless pillow fights.

My fondest memories of John, however, were the many times we played the songs we had written, and sang them together. I believe I was the first person to hear "I'm a Loser" as he was composing it right in front of me. He would ask me what I thought. I thought it was perfect.

By his example, and in his own words and music, he held the light that showed mankind how to reach for the best within itself. It was my good fortune to have been close to one of the brightest stars in the universe.

Jackie DeShannon is the singer-songwriter responsible for such pop standards as "Put a Little Love in Your Heart" and "What the World Needs Now Is Love."

The Greatest Rock 'N' Roll Love Story Ever Told

STEVE EARLE

I WAS NINE YEARS OLD IN FEBRUARY 1964 WHEN ED SULLIVAN INTRODUCED THE BEATLES TO AMERICA. IF I HAD LIVED IN NEW YORK OR L.A. PERHAPS I WOULD HAVE BEEN PREPARED FOR WHAT WAS GETTING READY TO HAPPEN TO me, but in tiny Converse, Texas, my world literally stood still that Sunday night and when it started spinning again on Monday morning nothing would ever be the same. At least not for me. I bought "She Loves You" the next day and every subsequent single as they were released. I had the fanzines, the model kits, the toy guitar, hell I even had a Beatle wig until the next-door neighbor's basset hound ate it. I found a community of preteen Beatles fans and we swapped records, paraphernalia and gossip.

Everybody had their favorite Beatle and I was no exception. In the beginning, I was a Paul guy. In those last innocent days before the Vietnam War became standard dinnertime fare on the evening news we only expected our heroes to be pop stars. Of the four, McCartney seemed to be the most comfortable in that skin. George and Ringo always seemed a little overwhelmed by all the hoopla they had created and John, beneath the class clown antics and the press conference wisecracks, was frankly a little scary. Darker and less accessible than the others.

Ironically, as I grew into an ambiguously iconoclastic, politically precocious teenager it was precisely that apparent discomfort and creative restlessness that attracted me to the enigma that was John. I read *In His Own Write* and traveled to Houston to see his "serious" acting debut in Richard Lester's *How I Won the War*. My Beatlemaniac friends at school were suspicious, even threatened by all of this extracurricular activity. They worried that too much individuality on the part of any one Beatle would compromise the solidarity of the group. I wasn't so sure about all that. I argued that John was the Beatle that walked his talk, constantly questioning everything he encountered in the rapidly changing world around him, including his own fame, fortune and Beatleness. My friends remained unconvinced. No matter how many times they listened to "Revolution" they were simply uncomfortable with the very concept of change when it came to the Boys from Liverpool. And then along came Yoko.

Everybody freaked. All of the Beatles had settled down by that time but the wives and girlfriends were only rarely seen in public. John and Yoko were inseparable; on the town, in the studio, in bed at the Amsterdam Hilton, even buck-ass-naked on the cover of *Two Virgins*. Beatles breakup rumors circulated all through 1968 while the faithful fidgeted and the press fed the mill. "She's gone to his head" indeed. When the word finally came in August 1969 that Paul McCartney had officially left the band, the Back Maskers, unable to deal with living in a world without a new Beatles album to decipher every Christmas, pounced. They needed a scapegoat and Yoko Ono was widely reviled as the Woman Who Broke Up the Beatles.

But not by me. Maybe it was my own contrarianism or maybe I was already entering the larval stage of the hopeless romantic I would eventually grow up to be. All I know is that the first time I saw a picture of John and Yoko together I was certain that I was witnessing nothing short of the Greatest Rock 'n' Roll Love Story Ever Told. From where I stood they seemed to literally complete each other, coming together as equals in a prototypical Aquarian life partnership. When they married, John took Yoko's name and from that day until he died they traveled hand in hand through the consciousness of a generation. They were no longer Ono or Lennon but simply John and Yoko, the first family of an alter-Camelot, a brief moment of our own when anything was possible and everything was open to discussion. Their life together became a shining example of what was possible when two people loved each other without condition or the constraint of traditional domestic roles. They were teaching us how to live up to our own ideals. How to be artists and activists and lovers and human beings. They said, "War is over if you want it," and some of us believed.

Those who didn't can be forgiven, I suppose, if you take into consideration the baggage of generations of sexism and, on this side of the pond, post–Pearl Harbor racism. They were predisposed to see only what they wanted to see. They limited themselves out of fear and prejudice, the Great Un-Equalizers. They triv-

ialized what they couldn't bring themselves to aspire to because it was too grand, too beautiful, too good to be true. They underestimated themselves, inevitably lowering their expectations.

But some of us got it. We watched John and Yoko, the greatest lovers of our time, devoted to each other and true to their dreams until the very end, and we saw just how powerful love really is.

Steve Earle is a singer/songwriter, author and activist. A much-sought-after speaker, he also hosts a nationally syndicated radio program.

BILL EPPRIDGE

I WAS ASSIGNED TO COVER THE BEATLES FOR A COUPLE OF DAYS DURING THEIR INTRODUCTION TO AMERICA IN FEBRUARY 1964. DURING THAT TIME, IT SEEMS THEY CAME TO UNDERSTAND WHO THEY WERE AND THEIR OWN IMPOR-tance in the music world. My job as a *Life* photographer was to photograph the Beatles as they really were, and not put myself into the pictures—to be invisible. John Lennon let me do that. The best thing he could have done for me was to ignore me. I really don't remember that he did anything special for me, which was exactly what I wanted.

I expected to see a pack of crazed deadbeats (the Beatles) but they weren't. They were four proper young gentlemen having a lot of fun with life and their new situation. Their popularity hit home at the Plaza Hotel when I left their suite and went out into the street with *Life* reporter Gail Cameron. Recognizing Gail as a member of the press, a group of young girls approached and asked if the Beatles had signed any autographs, and Gail said, "Yes." They looked at the pen in Gail's hand and asked her if any of the Beatles had used it to sign autographs, and Gail foolishly said, "Yes." She was knocked down by these screaming young girls. I ended up pulling them off her, and we had to run down the street to get away.

We took the train to the Washington, D.C., concert because of a bad snow-storm, and the Beatles made the most of it. They goofed the whole way down. The Beatles and the press had a private car. People from the rest of the train would come to our car to see the Lads . . . especially the young girls. And the Beatles obliged. John spent a lot of time looking out the train windows during the trip. They had never seen this country, and we had never seen them. I shot photographs, they shot quips, and history shot us all into the record books.

Bill Eppridge is a photojournalist who documented such subjects as the Vietnam War and Robert F. Kennedy's presidential campaign for *Life* magazine. In 1964 he photographed the Beatles on their first U.S. tour.

JOHN FOGERTY

I NEVER MET JOHN, BUT I ALWAYS FELT THAT I KNEW HIM. I'M SURE I SHARED THIS FEELING WITH MILLIONS OF PEOPLE AROUND THE WORLD. WHEN YOU REALLY LOVE SOMEONE'S CREATIVITY YOU LET THEM INTO YOUR HEART IN A very personal way. I remember the wonderful sense of discovery when the Beatles first arrived in America, as if I alone had found this amazing music. I believe we each had that feeling for a time.

Because I was also a musician, I paid attention to things perhaps differently than someone else might. For years, I felt that the Beatles just did everything right. I certainly tried to learn from their example.

For instance, the Beatles had evolved through the years into a four-piece band, emulating their idols, Buddy Holly and the Crickets. I still consider this perfection for Rock and Roll.

What I remember most about those early years was John Lennon's quick wit and irreverence toward the many sacred cows of old-fashioned society. He seemed to have been blessed with a natural intelligence that was totally unique in the rock-and-roll world.

You have to remember that before John Lennon and the Beatles, the expression of intelligence was decidedly uncool, especially in rock and roll. But at the same time, the Beatles always had reverence for the coolest icons of rock culture. Then they went on to do things that their heroes could never have imagined.

As time went on John expressed his vision in ever greater and wonderful ways. The famous bed-in with Yoko is simply remarkable and one of my favorites.

In the midst of the rebellious 1960s, *Revolution* was a record I particularly enjoyed on many levels. Besides being great music, it is the work of an ever-curious, restless spirit. At a time when he certainly could have pandered to the so-called counterculture, John instead questions the tendency by some to embrace "far-out" concepts simply because of their shock value. This is a lesson the young have to learn over and over.

But what has set John and the Beatles apart from everyone was possessing the artistic vision to break the mold and then having the musical and cultural depth to back it up.

John Lennon changed the world.

John Fogerty was lead singer, songwriter, guitarist and driving force behind Rock and Roll Hall of Famers Creedence Clearwater Revival. He has since enjoyed a long career as a solo artist and advocate for a variety of causes, including veterans' rights.

Peter Gabriel

How

like a big baby
you loved, and how you could love
you hurt, and knew how to hurt
you dreamed, and how you could dream
how I miss you.

Peter Gabriel is a founding member of art-rock band Genesis. He has received four Grammy Awards as a solo artist, including several for his pioneering work in the field of music video.

DAVID GEFFEN

EVEN TODAY, SOME FORTY YEARS AFTER THE FACT, I CAN HEAR A FEW BARS OF A BEATLES SONG AND BE IMMEDIATELY STRUCK BY THE TIMELESSNESS OF THE MUSIC AND THE SIGNIFICANCE OF THEIR LEGACY. I FIRST HEARD THEM IN 1963 and they affected me in a way that no other had before—I just kept listening to the music over and over again. I could also feel that they were more than a music group—they were true artists who kept expanding their horizons, taking all of us rapt listeners on a new journey with each album.

When I began my career in the music industry, I managed a lot of singer-songwriters, all of whom would happily admit their complete reverence for the writing talents of Lennon and McCartney and most of whom knew that for all their aspiration, they would never be on the level of the Beatles. When you are a singular force in the culture, your impact is indelible—so while the Beatles may have recorded their songs in the 1960s, their artistry defies the passing of time.

I first met John Lennon in 1974. He was recording an album with Phil Spector at A&M Records, and it was not a great time for him. He was separated from his wife, Yoko, at the time, and his life, both personally and professionally, was a mess. Six years later, Yoko reintroduced us and he was like a different person. He was sober and most important, he and Yoko had become parents. Having a child changed his life dramatically. He had never been one to embrace or deny his fame—he simply paid no attention to his celebrity. He and Yoko were parents first—and they succeeded in building a family life that was their first priority.

In 1980 both John and I were starting our careers again. I had just created Geffen Records and John was going into the recording studio with Yoko to record their album *Double Fantasy*. I knew it would be quite a coup to sign them, but I didn't think I had a chance. I wrote Yoko a letter—because I knew that the only person who could make it happen was her. John had complete faith in her; he trusted her in all decisions about business. His motive in recording *Double Fantasy* was completely romantic in that he wanted the record to show the world Yoko's talents and for his wife to finally get the recognition he felt she deserved. He wanted the light to shine on her. "We have to take care of Yoko," he would say to me. "That is our goal with this record."

Yoko, however, was a pragmatist and she would tell him that the public wanted to hear him, not her. But he wouldn't hear it. He was her biggest fan. Their marriage was a true partnership, rooted in deep respect and total faith in each other. I have been involved with stars my whole adult life, but I do not think I have ever known another couple so clearly two halves of a whole.

So we made the record. John and Yoko were thrilled with its success and excited that the world was embracing their work together. And then, in the passing of a few minutes, on a busy New York street, one man took it all away . . . from them, and us.

I don't like to think or talk about the night John was killed. When I first got the call from someone who told me to go to the hospital to meet Yoko—that John had been shot—I thought it was a crank call. When the horrible reality hit me, I went to the hospital—and stayed with her. The doctor wanted me to tell her that John was dead, but I just couldn't do it. I begged him to tell her.

When we came back to the Dakota that night, pinned to their door was a pullout quadruple fold of the Billboard top one hundred chart. The record was number nine and John had circled it and added an arrow pointing up to number one. And of course, it went to number one the very next week.

Since that horrible night, I have remained a friend and admirer of Yoko's. We all lost something when we lost John and even today I miss his music, his spirit and his ambition to live and raise his family in a world at peace. Yoko lost all of this and so much more. He, along with their son, will always be her true loves. But I know one thing for sure—whether it is his Beatles stuff or a piece of poetry like "Imagine," which is my favorite John Lennon song, the art he created will be appreciated long after all of us are gone.

David Geffen founded the Asylum and Geffen record labels before turning his attention to film production with Dreamworks SKG. John Lennon and Yoko Ono's *Double Fantasy* was the second release on the Geffen label in November 1980.

JULIE GOLD

I was eight years old when the Beatles played the *Ed Sullivan Show* back in 1964.

My life changed forever that night.

I remember when the camera zoomed in on John Lennon and this ticker was underneath him saying something like, "Sorry girls, he's married. . . ."

I wasn't jealous, I just hoped his wife loved him as much as I did.

For forty years I've loved him.

Most of those forty years I've surrounded myself with his music, his message and always photos of him.

I've slept under his portrait most of my life.

I remember when Elvis Presley died and the news had all these images of people crying around the world.

I could not identify with those people, but I remember asking God to please never ever let anything bad happen to John Lennon, because then I'd be crying, too.

Forever.

I wanted John Lennon to outlive me.

I remember when Yoko came into the picture and everyone was mad at her.

I didn't get it.

After all, in my opinion, she brought out the best in John.

It was the word "yes" that triggered their romance.

He wrote his best music and became the most outspoken "under her influence."

For my sixteenth birthday a friend gave me Yoko's book, entitled *Grapefruit*.

I loved it.

I loved Yoko.

When I was in high school John and Yoko hosted the *Mike Douglas Show*, which was shot in my hometown of Philadelphia.

I remember our local paper had a photo of the two of them walking down Walnut Street carrying a small drum they had bought in a store I frequented.

It was surreal for me.

How could they actually be in my city?

I guess I didn't think of them as human.

They gave too much to the world to be merely human.

As a New Yorker I would occasionally walk past the Dakota, though I could not grasp the reality of the two of them actually living there and walking in and out of that majestic building.

December 8, 1980. I'd been in New York two years.

I went to sleep early that night.

I was awakened abruptly when my phone started ringing and ringing.

All calls from my Philadelphia friends.

"Did you hear the news?" "Turn on your TV. . . ."

There was a football game on. There was a ticker under the game.

It was about John Lennon being shot.

Then Howard Cosell made the horrifying announcement.

Once again, my life changed forever.

Who could kill John Lennon?

How was that possible?

Why did God ignore my prayer?

How could I ever listen to the Beatles again?

How can I live without knowing that somewhere in the world John Lennon is Alive?

Julie Gold

The pain has never gone away.

I still cry.

I still read Yoko's poem "Season of Glass."

I saw Yoko sometime in 1981 or 1982. She was walking down Broadway.

I wanted to say hello, but I didn't want to intrude on her privacy.

I knew that if John hadn't been killed, that would have been the time I got to see them together in person. I framed the image in my soul.

I imagined him beside her.

Just before my fortieth birthday, I decided to take a chance and write to Yoko.

I just needed to tell her I loved her.

To thank her.

To tell her about getting *Grapefruit* for my sixteenth birthday and now turning forty.

Writing to her was a cathartic experience. I didn't know if she'd ever even read my letter; still, it was something I had to do.

A few months later I got this envelope in the mail. The return address said Studio One. I didn't have a clue.

I opened the envelope and there was a postcard of John and Yoko during their "Two Gurus in Bed" period; their "bed-in" for peace.

It was signed "To Julie, In Sisterhood. Love X Yoko NYC '96."

It is framed by my front door (under a sacred letter from Carole King).

I see it every day of my life when I come and go.

It gives me courage, strength, hope, happiness.

I cherish that photo.

In 1985 I wrote "From a Distance."

I know that my songwriting is completely influenced by the Beatles.

I know every word they ever sang.

I know every note they ever played.

It's in my blood. It's part of who I am.

Musically, there can be no finer teacher than the Beatles.

I've been blessed to live my life now as a rewarded and respected musician.

I thank God daily for my blessed life and the abundance of gifts therein.

At the end of my daily prayers I talk to a few choice people:

My Father.

John Lennon.

Laura Nyro.

Martin Luther King.

John F. Kennedy.

Robert F. Kennedy.

I thank them daily for the positive influence they had and continue to have on my life and my music.

They're with me daily.

As for John, I have his self-portrait over my bed and his beautiful drawing of him and Yoko next to my piano.

It's right next to a Paul McCartney print, signed by Paul.

How can I not be inspired when I'm at my piano with the Beautiful Hudson River of Dreams just outside my window?

And so, the final part of my story unfolds. . . .

Every few years Yoko Ono has an art show somewhere in New York.

I always go, and it never disappoints.

So I saw a notice that she was going to exhibit some of John's work at a gallery down in SoHo for a few days in October, including October 9, which would have been his sixty-fourth birthday.

I put on my Yellow Submarine T-shirt.

I put on my "Imagine Peace" button which I got at a Yoko art show last year.

I always have my Imagine lucky stone in my pocket.

And then I walked down to SoHo.

As expected, it was an emotional experience to be there surrounded by his paintings, his drawings, his song lyrics, photos of him, videos of him.

There was a sense of kinship among all of us milling around.

A palpable sense of loss, love, nostalgia, inevitability.

I found my way to the back of the exhibit and stood before a silent video of my fallen hero playing "Imagine" on that white grand piano with Yoko looking on in the background.

I remember first seeing those images when they were new.

I remember hearing "Imagine" for the first time and how deeply it touched me and changed me.

I was lost in the moment.

Reverie.

Sorrow.

Prayer.

I sensed a presence next to me.

I heard a slight sigh.

I looked up.

Yoko.

It was Yoko standing next to me in an art gallery in SoHo staring up at an image of her beloved husband; my beloved idol.

I think I sucked most of the air out of the room when I exclaimed "Yoko . . ."

I didn't know exactly what to say but I think and hope that the love I felt at that moment was transmitted.

I took my Imagine stone out of my pocket and showed her.

I pointed to my "Imagine Peace" button.

And with every ounce of love and sincerity that I have ever felt, I said, "Thank you, Yoko. Thank you."

We hugged each other.

She thanked me, too, and wished me luck.

I just stood there as she wandered off and was suddenly surrounded by autograph seekers and photo opportunities.

I kept watching the video of John.

I sensed that he was right there with us.

I bought a T-shirt with his image.

I walked home through SoHo, weeping.

That is my story. It really happened.

I did not imagine it, though I still Imagine.

I still "Imagine the Clouds Dripping."

I still know that Love Is All You Need.

Yoko Ono is somewhere in New York City. For one magical moment, our lives intersected and our energies meshed.

I told John all about it the very next day.

He already knew.

SEASON OF GLASS

spring passes
and one remembers one's innocence
summer passes
and one remembers one's exuberance
autumn passes
and one remembers one's reverence
winter passes
and one remembers one's perseverance
there is a season that never passes and that is the season of glass

Julie Gold is a singer/songwriter who also tours periodically as a member of the Four Bitchin' Babes. Her composition "From a Distance" won the 1990 Grammy for Song of the Year.

BOB GOMEL

THE YEAR WAS 1964. LIFE MAGAZINE ASSIGNED ME TO PHO-
TOGRAPH THE BEATLES ON THEIR VISIT TO MIAMI. I
ARRANGED FOR A PHOTO SHOOT AT THE DEAUVILLE HOTEL,
WHERE *THE ED SULLIVAN SHOW* WOULD BE BROADCAST,
but the hysteria of Beatlemania required a change of plans. Comedian
Myron Cohen came to my rescue. He arranged an alternative location
at the celebrity home of Paul and Jerri Pollack.

The Beatles showed up in two convertibles with their manager, Brian
Epstein. My first impression of the guys was how polite they were. They
seemed uncertain how to react. They waited to be told what to do.

After changing into matching bathing suits, four pale, skinny guys
entered the pool. I asked them to just have fun. Ringo started a splash
fight. John did a few cannonballs off the diving board. That captured
moment became my favorite photograph. It hangs in my gallery today.

There are other memories of my limited experience with the Beatles:
at the Sullivan show, on the beach, etc., but it was the private session at
the pool that stands out. They were extremely polite and very, very pale.

Bob Gomel was a staff photographer at *Life* magazine, where he worked with an array of prominent figures until his departure to enter the field of advertising in 1969. In 1964 he was one of several photographers selected to document the Beatles' first U.S. tour.

HARRY GOODWIN

I WAS BROUGHT UP IN THE INDUSTRIAL NORTH OF ENGLAND, NOT VERY FAR FROM LIVERPOOL, THE HOME OF JOHN LENNON. BRITISH ROCK WAS STILL IN ITS INFANCY WHEN I LANDED A JOB WITH A NEW BBC TELEVISION PRODUCTION, *Top of the Pops,* devised and originally aired in an old converted church in Manchester. No one speculated back then how huge this show was to become. This was the north of England, far from the bustle of London, with its recording studios, pop news publications and music moguls. Two years later, however, the show was relocated to a London BBC Television studio.

I went out one evening in 1963 and headed to the Odeon Cinema in Manchester in search of some good shots of the Beatles; I wasn't really focused on photographing the main name act of the evening. The Beatles were, by this time, already pretty well established especially in the northwest of England, and since they were appearing in my hometown, I was enthusiastic to meet them and get them in front of my camera for the first time. Brian Bint, the Odeon's manager at the time and someone I knew, let me in before the show began, so I could find the group and photograph them backstage. I found the Beatles in a dressing room and from the first moment, John's dry northern English humor and my streetwise background clicked together. "Who else that's important have you photographed?" John asked me in a challenging manner. "How about Chuck Berry? He's even been to my house for tea and toast; is that good enough?" I answered. "Good enough for me. Let's go then," John retorted. I didn't know at the time but John was a long-standing fan of Chuck Berry. After that exchange, they were very cooperative in allowing me to take pictures. John, who was known for his off-the-cuff dry humor, showed his willingness to give me a special accommodation to get the pictures I came for.

The Beatles already had an established fan base and some of the girls had put together a large card with messages of good luck for the Beatles' Manchester appearance. After some small talk with the group and simultaneous to their reading the fans' card, I decided to move in for my first shot. Something on the card which was of a humorous, sexually suggestive nature caught John's attention, and a slightly astonished John yelled to me to take a look at what someone had written. At that precise moment, I snapped the picture with John looking right at me and pointing to the card. This was the first picture I ever took of the Beatles, and to this day I feel it to be very special, as it captures John's essence. I took several additional photos and got to know the group more, but regrettably was limited to three or four shots by Brian Epstein, their manager.

Another notable meeting with John came in 1965, at the Apollo Theatre in Ardwick, Manchester. The "Fab Four," as the Beatles were affectionately known, had a one-nighter in Manchester, and the fans were out in full force. It was a bizarre evening all around. There was a strike on in Manchester which caused some interruptions of local services, including electricity and public transportation. It wasn't known up until the last moment if the show would go on, and the fans were uneasy, to say the least. I, together with a few other photographers, was positioned in the orchestra stalls, right in front of the stage. As soon as the group began, the fans started throwing Jelly Babies (a British soft candy about an inch or so long). Their aim for the stage on many occasions fell short and hit the photographers on their heads. This wasn't so bad, but when the candies ran out the audience started tossing coins, some from as high as the upper circle seating area two floors above. The photographers were in direct line of the coins that fell short of the stage. John knew me well by this time and saw what was going on. He found humor in the situation, and repeatedly made eye contact with me and laughed. I admit it must have been

May 30, 1963.

April 7, 1965, at Riverside BBC Studios in Hammersmith, London, to promote the U.K. release of "Ticket to Ride."

Early 1966, in the dressing room at *Top of the Pops*.

an amusing sight to John, but at the time it didn't seem that way. I decided finally it was too dangerous and gave up the position to another photographer. John made it up to me, however, as soon as the show was over by sending word for me to come to the dressing room. I was the first, and maybe the only, photographer who got to take posed pictures of the Beatles that evening because of John's help.

By this time, I was well known to the Beatles as the resident *Top of the Pops* photographer; the show was by then a very important television pop production. The show aired live every Thursday evening, but sometimes the planned appearance of the Beatles would be in conflict with another engagement they had. Not wanting to miss them being included in the show when the group was at number one, the producer Johnny Stewart would plan a taping session on another day so he had the footage for his show. I would go to the studio and take pictures which could be projected onto a screen during the live show as an added feature. Sometimes John was reluctant to be repeatedly photographed, but saw the benefit of the show having pictures to maximize their publicity. There was a constant need for new pictures for the BBC production.

On one occasion when the Beatles were appearing live on the show, it was hard because of their security agents to get into their dressing room for a picture. That particular show night, as they came offstage they were escorted with one bodyguard in front, then the four Beatles, with another bodyguard in the rear. Somehow, I managed to slip in after the fourth Beatle and in front of the bodyguard and made it into the dressing room. John was astonished and upset to see me breach the secure line. "How did you get in here?" John yelled. Paul intervened, pointing out how important it was to have pictures for the show while the group was away in the United States. John then saw the obvious benefit and apologized for his original reaction. John had a good heart and always treated me fairly, even though our dialogue was of a sparring nature.

The last time I photographed John was the result of a 5:00 PM press call in 1970. John and Yoko were at *Top of the Pops* for the release of "Instant Karma." It had been a couple of years since our last meeting. Some of the other photographers asked me to put a good word in for them with John, which I did. I asked John, "Do you remember me?" John without hesitation replied, "When do you want to do pictures?" John added, "Do your press pictures, and then I will send Mark, my assistant, to get you for a private session in my dressing room suite." John was married

to Yoko, and she accompanied him to the session. "Yoko, this is Harry Goodwin, the 'official' pop photographer; the ultimate! How long on *Top of the Pops,* Harry?" "Seven years now, John," I replied. I was with the show another two years after that day. I warmly remember that introduction to Yoko and John's sincerity.

I was impressed by John's maturity and the way his demeanor had changed from the fresh-faced rebel I had originally encountered in the early 1960s. It was amazing how pleasantly his manner had developed. I did a wonderful and extensive photo session which included many posed portraits of John and pictures with Yoko. One picture from this session was used to represent John in a television program lasting over a ten-week period. The show was to judge by viewer participation the "Ten Greatest Britons." It was a BBC Television production in cooperation with the London National Portrait Gallery. Winston Churchill was voted number one. John Lennon came in number seven, chosen from an array of very important people both present-day and historical. A book was published about the program and overseen by the National Portrait Gallery curator, Mr. Terrence Pepper. My photo of John wearing the denim shirt and "people for peace" message on the sleeve is featured in the book and exhibited in the Gallery.

During this last photo session, we fondly reminisced on the old days of the Beatles. "Remember getting twenty-five pounds [approx $50] for your first show on Granada Television's *People and Places* in 1964, John? The canceled check is displayed proudly on the wall of the press office at Granada Television today!" I told him. I also mentioned another incident from 1964 when I used one of John's pictures as part of my first assignment for *Top of the Pops.* Prior to this, the show had used cutouts from newspapers of artists to project onto the backdrop of the stage; I received special recognition from the producer because of this picture. I expressed to John that day how very grateful I was for all the help he had given me over the years.

A wonderful selection of photos from that last session is precious to me and always will be.

I never saw John again after that day.

Harry Goodwin is a photographer who has captured hundreds of famous faces, including the Beatles, in a career spanning fifty years. He has often been called "photographer to the stars," and was house photographer for the British television show *Top of the Pops* from 1964 to 1973.

BOB GRUEN

I ALWAYS FELT VERY FORTUNATE TO HAVE MET AND KNOWN JOHN LENNON. I ALWAYS HAD A GOOD TIME WHEN I WAS WITH HIM. HE WAS VERY PERCEPTIVE, INTELLIGENT AND FUNNY.

I first saw him in 1971 at the Apollo Theater in New York at a benefit and remember it as one of the most exciting moments I've experienced.

We actually met for the first time in the spring of 1972, when I was on a photo assignment. John and Yoko liked the photos I made that night; they used one in the *Sometime in New York City* album package, and I started working with them more regularly.

John and Yoko were each powerful, creative media artists, and I was always thrilled to be a part of their team. They were very much in touch with each other, and that seemed to combine their strengths. I learned a lot from them as they expressed in song, writings and artworks their feelings of love, fear, anger, loneliness, jealousy and lust; they were open about everything. Their concert at Madison Square Garden was fantastic, but critics who expected Beatle music were shocked by the outspoken political and feminist ideas they presented.

John went through a lot of changes while I knew him. In the early

1970s there was a lot of drinking and carrying on. In 1973–74 there was a "lost weekend" period, but then he reconnected with Yoko and spent the next five years raising their son, Sean, and learning to live a more sober, responsible life. When Sean was one month old John called me to take photos for his family, and I remember that day as the happiest I'd ever seen him.

When he went back in the studio in 1980 he seemed to have really clear ideas about life. In his conversations and the interviews he gave at this time, he talked a lot about commitment, parenting and health, ideas that were to become popular themes of today.

Bob Gruen is one of the most well-known and respected photographers in rock and roll. From Muddy Waters to the Rolling Stones, Elvis to Madonna, Bob Dylan to Bob Marley, he has captured the music scene for more than forty years, and today his work is known around the world. His most recent published work includes *The Clash: Photographs by Bob Gruen* and *John Lennon: The New York Years.*

Yoko and John at New York's Apollo Theater, December 17, 1971.

John and Yoko were about to leave the Apollo Theater after their appearance at the benefit for the families of prisoners hurt in the Attica Prison uprising. A number of people were taking snapshots of them, so I took a few pictures myself. John said, "People are taking our pictures all the time, and we never get to see them." I told him I lived around the corner from him and I would be glad to show him mine, and a few days later I dropped them off. We didn't actually meet until several months after that.

John and Yoko at the St. Regis Hotel, New York City, spring 1972.

Henry Edwards was writing an article for *After Dark* magazine about the band Elephant's Memory, who were working at the time as John and Yoko's backing band. Henry asked me to come to take pictures of John and Yoko when he interviewed them for the story. After the interview I asked if I could come along to the studio to take pictures of them all working together. They liked the pictures I took that night, used one in their album package for *Sometime in New York City* and asked me to stay in touch and work with them.

Bob Gruen

John and Yoko agreed to appear at a benefit concert at Madison Square Garden and the rehearsals were held at the closed Fillmore East theater. I was impressed by how much John and Yoko were in touch with each other, both physically and mentally. As the preparations got busier and more and more people swirled around them, John and Yoko seemed like the grounded center of all the activity.

John and Yoko at rehearsals in Fillmore East, New York City, August 1972.

The concert at Madison Square Garden was one of the most exciting I've ever been to. All the musicians had a background of rollicking fifties' style rock and roll and John and Yoko's songs were all really meaningful. The audience was impressed by the power of their message. Watching John sing "Imagine" was a moment I'll never forget.

Above: Harry Nilsson and John Lennon play pool at Record Plant Studio, New York City, April 1974.
Opposite: John Lennon at Madison Square Garden, New York City, August 30, 1972.

John was producing Harry Nilsson's *Pussy Cats* album at the Record Plant studio in New York. When I dropped by they were taking a break, playing pool. Many of Harry's songs are sweet and romantic, but Harry had a wild side as well. He and John spent a lot of time barhopping and having fun.

John Lennon, New York City, August 28, 1974.

John asked me to come to his penthouse apartment to take portrait photos for the cover of his *Walls and Bridges* album. After shooting a series for the album we took some more pictures to have available for publicity. Since we were on a roof surrounded by the city, I asked John if he still had the shirt I had given him a year earlier with "New York City" printed on it. He went and got it, and we took this picture, which has since become one of the most widely published images of John Lennon.

Bob Gruen

The U.S. government was trying to deport John Lennon, and I thought a good image to support his case for staying here would be to show him with the Statue of Liberty, the symbol of welcome to the United States. John agreed, and we took the regular tourist ferry out to Liberty Island, walked around in front of the statue and took a few rolls of pictures. This is one of my favorite pictures. I feel that John Lennon and the Statue of Liberty both represent the desire for personal freedom.

John Lennon, Statue of Liberty, New York City, October 30, 1974.

A month after Sean was born, John called and asked me to take family pictures. When I arrived they were all dressed in formal kimonos for the photo. John was happier than I'd ever seen him and was enjoying his relationship with his new son.

John, Yoko and Sean, at the Dakota apartments, New York City, November 1975.

John and Yoko, Record Plant studio, New York City, December 5, 1980.

In December 1980 I went to the Record Plant, where John and Yoko were mixing Yoko's new record, *Walking on Thin Ice*. When they finished working we took some pictures around the studio, and I asked them to pose in front of a giant guitar that John had made for their "This Is Not Here" art exhibit at the Everson Museum in Syracuse. They posed facing the camera for a few shots and then John pushed Yoko against the wall, wrapping himself around her saying, "Get a picture of this! This is what people want to see!"

I stayed up till dawn talking to John at the Record Plant. He was very excited that their new record *Double Fantasy* was selling well and that the single "Starting Over" looked like it would go to number one. He was very much looking forward to a planned world tour. We talked about where we would shop in Tokyo and where we would eat in Paris. He seemed to be clearer and stronger than I had ever seen him.

John and Yoko in front of Record Plant studio, Forty-fourth Street, New York City, December 6, 1980.

Ronnie Hawkins

In December 1969 John and Yoko were fully committed to their War Is Over If You Want It peace campaign. When I got the phone call from London that they were coming to stay with me, I was thrilled, though I admit I didn't know that much about the Beatles personally. I just knew about all the hits they had played on the radio. I was a bar act back in 1969, playing the current popular songs every night. I had a band working with me called Robbie Lane and the Disciples, and they learned all the Beatles and Rolling Stones and all that other Limey stuff. Still, while I knew their songs were big, I didn't have any earthly idea that the Beatles were going to stay around as long as they did. Anyone else in the world having had that happen would have just done cartwheels and started biting themselves in the arse.

When they arrived, I thought I've got to get into them a little bit. See where these big-time people were at. In the case of Yoko, she was educated. She could speak four or five languages and she was phoning everybody in the world from the ambassador of Japan to Princess Margaret and Peter Sellers. And John was an absolutely wonderful cat, unbelievable. I just observed him and his whole attitude, his whole thing on life. He just seemed to be a real good guy. He wasn't conning people in any way. He was very gifted in some special sort of way. And I didn't realize how powerful he was. John would reach for a cigarette and seventeen lighters came out. It was like the sprinkler system coming on at a golf course.

While John was signing his *Bag One* lithographs, somebody managed to slip on a copy of my new album, which I'd recorded in Muscle Shoals a couple of months earlier under the production genius of Jerry Wexler. And it turned out that John liked it a lot, especially the version of the old Clovers' hit "Down in the Alley," which Jerry Wexler had recorded in its original version. But I must say that I didn't take advantage of anything because I didn't want to bug them. At the time, it seemed like everyone was trying to mooch off John.

I gave them the best of everything I had because they were the stars. My wife, Wanda, and I moved out of our master bedroom for them. Of course, I didn't know at the time that they were going to get stoned, pass out and turn the bathwater on, which overflowed and resulted in the brand-new ceiling caving in on us. Nor did I know that somebody would manage to set the garage on fire. Or that fans would be climbing over the fence to catch a glimpse of John. Our security guy, Heavy Andrews, was charged with assault for chasing off a journalist who'd been trespassing.

In the meantime, it was funny how I suddenly got all of my friends back. I did my best to keep them away from John, but the media I couldn't control. You wouldn't believe the number of people who rang me up and pretended they didn't know that John and Yoko were staying there.

Macrobiotic cooks were brought in to prepare John and Yoko's special food. Despite that diet, I caught John and Yoko down at the fridge a couple of times in the middle of the night having a quick slice of bologna.

At that time, the Beatles had already broken up. But nobody knew about that yet. We knew about it because we heard them talking on the phone about things to do with the Beatles. I mean, I hadn't kept up with the Beatles personally at all. I didn't know anything about John's private life. Or Yoko's private life. Until they came to my house and told me all that shit about how that Indian guru was chasing those teenage girls.

Wanda and I accompanied John and Yoko and the whole peace party in the private train carriage to Ottawa for the historic meeting with Prime Minister

A group traveled in a private railway observation car from Toronto to Ottawa, Canada, to meet with Prime Minister Pierre Trudeau in December 1969. Left to right: John Lennon, Yoko Ono, Anthony Fawcett (kneeling), John Brower (promoter), Wanda Hawkins, Ronnie Hawkins, and Ritchie Yorke.

Pierre Trudeau. That was wonderful, man. I'd never been on one of those private coaches ever. I didn't even know they existed. It was like the party that President Clinton threw for me in Toronto in 2002. I didn't know that there were suites like that. I'd never been in one before. I mean, twenty-four-hour room service. Two master suites. I could remain on the road forever if I could stay in one of those private carriages.

During the meeting with the prime minister, I wasn't paying too much attention. Wanda and I were just tagging along on that trip and seeing unbelievable things. To meet Pierre Trudeau and all those people, to eat at those unbelievable restaurants—it was mind-blowing. And then on the plane flight back to Toronto from Ottawa, with the former Prime Minister Lester Pearson on board. That was very special, too.

When I heard about John being shot, I was back in Arkansas. I'd gone down there to visit my mum and dad. Within five minutes, I had the U.S. TV networks onto me wanting comments. It was a terrible time for any of us who'd had the great pleasure of meeting John.

Ronnie Hawkins is founder and lead singer of rock-and-roll legends the Hawks (later the Band). His close friendship with John Lennon and Yoko Ono led to several peace-related projects, including the 1970 "Love Not War" world tour.

Enemy of the State: The Secret War Against John Lennon

TOM HAYDEN

JOHN LENNON CANNOT BE MEMORIALIZED WITHOUT RECALLING HIS RADICAL POLITICAL ATTITUDES AT A TIME OF ROILING UNREST IN BRITAIN, AMERICA AND AROUND THE GLOBE. HIS GREATEST QUALITIES WERE AS AN ARTIST, of course, but he would have been a different artist without the rebellious, nonconformist and subversive spirit of the 1960s. Revered by all as a great musician, John also became an enemy of the state, which future generations of fans need to remember.

The forces who targeted John Lennon—some combination of London's MI5 and J. Edgar Hoover's FBI—did so clandestinely, then waged a further war to keep their embarrassing improprieties hidden and impeccable reputations intact.

Their counterintelligence campaign unfolded, as far as we know, as the Beatles evolved from an entertainment sensation to a fountainhead of a counterculture consciousness to a formidable political threat in the person of John Lennon.

Five years after the Beatles had performed a last time in San Francisco in 1966, Lennon performed a live concert in December 1971 in Ann Arbor, Michigan. His "Give Peace a Chance" was already a peace anthem. But this cause had a harder edge, a benefit for imprisoned musician-turned-revolutionary John Sinclair. The flower children of Motown were becoming "white panthers," consciously emulating the Black Panther Party. According to the FBI documents obtained in a lawsuit by the historian Jon Wiener, FBI agents were in the audience of fifteen thousand that night and did not like what they heard, saw or inhaled. For years the spy agency had been frustrated by the rise of a counterculture; one 1966 strategy memo lamented that the "nonconformism in dress and speech, neglect of personal cleanliness, use of obscenities (printed and uttered), publicized sexual promiscuity, experimenting with and the use of drugs, filthy clothes, shaggy hair, wearing of sandals, beads and unusual jewelry *tend to negate any attempt to hold these people up to ridicule*" (emphasis added; SAC, Newark, to Director, FBI, Memorandum, May 27, 1968 [Counterintelligence Program, Internal Security: Disruption of the New Left/Re Bureau letter to Albany], 5/10/63).

Declassified cable traffic reveals that the key reason the Bureau attempted to deport John and Yoko Lennon in early 1972 for overstaying a visa was not a prior marijuana charge in London, but the upcoming 1972 reelection campaign of Richard Nixon. Antiwar sentiment had reached majority proportions in America and activism had acquired a militant edge with the siege of the White House and thousands of arrests in May 1971. Nixon's paranoia was seemingly boundless. That same year he illegally authorized the White House "plumbers" to ransack the Democratic National Committee offices in Washington, steal confidential files from Daniel Ellsberg's therapist, and lay plans to suppress the planned protests at the Republican National Convention in San Diego.

John Lennon and Yoko Ono figured prominently in the plans and dreams of those hoping to upset Nixon that year. "A confidential source who has furnished reliable information in the past" advised the FBI that Lennon gave $75,000 in early 1972 toward a plan to "disrupt the Republican National Convention."

On March 1, another "confidential source" advised that I had flown into Washington for a secret meeting with Rennie Davis to discuss an election-year plan involving demonstrations, speaking tours and a New Left–oriented "entertainment group" composed of John and Yoko, whose "function [was] a stimulus to encourage youths to be in the vicinity of election candidates when they are on tour" (FBI memorandum [Election Year Strategy Information Center], March 8, 1972).

On March 16, 1972, another FBI memo warned that "subject" Lennon "continues to plan activities directed towards RNC and will soon initiate series of 'rock concerts' to develop financial support. . . ." The agent advised that the New York Bureau "promptly initiate discreet efforts to locate subject" and that any information linking Lennon to drugs be "immediately furnished to Bureau in form suitable for dissemination."

On May 21, the Bureau pledged to *"neutralize any disruptive activities of subject,"* (emphasis added) in the chilling vocabulary of the FBI's counterintelligence (COINTEL) program (Jon Wiener, *Gimme Some Truth,* University of California Press, 1999, p. 238).

Somewhere between fantasy and reality, Rennie was convinced that John Lennon could transcend and unify our fragmented world with one more grand tour of protest. Abbie Hoffman and Jerry Rubin shared the same dream, and were meeting with Lennon, Rennie said. It was a time of grand and distrustful egotisms, however, despite the considerable expansion of public support for the movement's aims of peace and tolerance. One reason is that Nixon was withdrawing ground troops from Vietnam while continuing the bombing, sending police after the Black Panthers and their friends, and indicting up to sixty separate antiwar protestors on various conspiracy charges. All this was causing activists to wonder and quarrel about whether the long war was ending or heating up. One can only speculate about the role that FBI counterintelligence programs, and the plentitude of drugs, played in fostering this paranoia.

The Lennons were consumed in their government-triggered deportation hearings and could not imagine being at the storm center of a six-month crusade of concerts and confrontations to dump Richard Nixon. They would speak out, and did, being photographed in conical hats showing solidarity with South Vietnamese political prisoners. He and Yoko endorsed a protest that resulted in cancellation of the annual Armed Forces Day in New York City (Wiener, 266). But on their deportation lawyer's advice, they dropped the convention concert plans by the end of 1971.

The whole bizarre history surrounding that convention remains to be told. Later documents would show that G. Gordon Liddy (of Watergate infamy) took part in a planning group that considered kidnapping protest leaders and dumping us in the Mexican desert. A vigilante group called the Secret Army Organization (SAO) took shots into a San Diego house filled with protest planners; one bullet pierced a wrist. An FBI undercover agent sat in the car next to the shooter.

Airtel

~~CONFIDENTIAL~~   4/10/72

To: SAC, New York   (100-175319)   (Enclosures - 2)

From: Director, FBI   (100-469910)   1 - Mr. Horner
                                                   1 - Mr. Preusse
JOHN WINSTON LENNON   1 - Mr. Shackelford
SM - NEW LEFT   1 - Mr. Pence

        ReNYtel 3/16/72.

            Enclosed for information of New York are two copies of
Alexandria airtel dated 3/31/72 captioned "White Panther Party,
IS - WPP; CALREP; MIDEM," which contains information from Alexandria
source relating to current activities of subject.

            It appears from referenced New York teletype that subject
and wife might be preparing for lengthy delaying tactics to avert
their deportation in the near future. In the interim, very real
possibility exists that subject, as indicated in enclosed airtel,
might engage in activities in U.S. leading toward disruption of
Republican National Convention (RNC), San Diego, 8/72. For this
reason New York promptly initiate discreet efforts to locate subject
and remain aware of his activities and movements. Handle inquiries
only through established sources and discreet pretext inquiries.
Careful attention should be given to reports that subject is heavy
narcotics user and any information developed in this regard should be
furnished to narcotics authorities and immediately furnished to
Bureau in form suitable for dissemination.

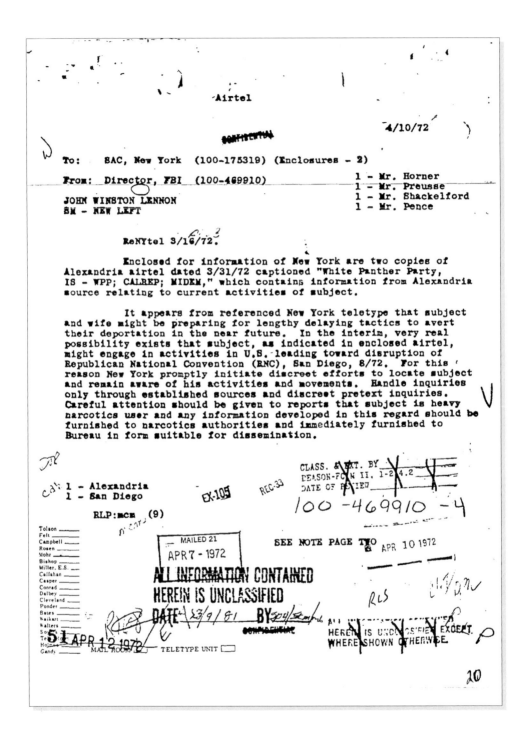

        1 - Alexandria
        1 - San Diego   EX-105   REC-33

        RLP:mcb   (9)   100-469910-4

Tolson ___
Felt ___
Campbell ___   MAILED 21   SEE NOTE PAGE TWO   APR 10 1972
Rosen ___   APR 7 - 1972
Mohr ___
Bishop ___   ALL INFORMATION CONTAINED
Miller, E.S. ___
Callahan ___   HEREIN IS UNCLASSIFIED
Casper ___
Conrad ___   DATE 23/9/81 BY 504/smib
Dalbey ___
Cleveland ___   ~~CONFIDENTIAL~~
Ponder ___
Bates ___
Waikart ___
Walters ___   ALL INFORMATION CONTAINED
Soyars ___   HEREIN IS UNCLASSIFIED EXCEPT
5 APR 12 1972   WHERE SHOWN OTHERWISE.
Holmes ___
Gandy ___   MAIL ROOM ___ TELETYPE UNIT ___

                                                                        10

Airtel to New York'
RE: John Winston Lennon
100-469910

     In view of subject's avowed intention to engage in
disruptive activities surrounding RNC, New York Office will be
responsible for closely following his activities until time of
actual deportation. Afford this matter close supervision and
keep Bureau fully advised by most expeditious means warranted.

NOTE:

     John Lennon, former member of Beatles singing group,
is allegedly in U.S. to assist in organizing disruption of RNC.
Due to narcotics conviction in England, he is being deported
along with wife Yoko Ono. They appeared at Immigration and
Naturalization Service, New York, 3/16/72, for deportation
proceedings but won delay until 4/18/72 because subject fighting
narcotics conviction and wife fighting custody child case in
U.S. Strong possibility looms that subject will not be deported
any time soon and will probably be in U.S. at least until RNC.
Information developed by Alexandria source that subject continues
to plan activities directed toward RNC and will soon initiate
series of "rock concerts" to develop financial support with
first concert to be held Ann Arbor, Michigan, in near future.
New York Office covering subject's temporary residence and
being instructed to intensify discreet investigation of subject to
determine activities vis a vis RNC.

21

F B I

INDEX ENCL.

Transmit in _____ Via _____ Airtel _____

(Type in plaintext or code)   (Priority)

Date ___ 9/19/73

To: SAC, New York

From: Director, FBI

ELSUR
JOHN WINSTON ONO LENNON

BUDED: 9/24/73

        Enclosed for your office is one copy of Department
of Justice memorandum dated 9/18/73 requesting electronic
surveillance information in accordance with specific questions
set forth in the enclosed memorandum.

        Conduct check in order to answer specific questions
in enclosed memorandum and Criminal Division memorandum,
4/16/69, furnished field 5/2/69. Key answers to correspond
with questions A through F. If results reveal positive
information, insure microphone sources monitoring individuals
involved are identified to the Bureau.

        New York check captioned individual.

        Sutel your response to reach Bureau by COB 9/24/73.
If positive, submit logs and pertinent documents by airtel.

Enclosure

ALL INFORMATION CONTAINED
HEREIN IS UNCLASSIFIED
DATE 16 78 REP P/cam : 5-2-83

(Do not type below this line.) 92-4564-2651

b7C

SEARCHED_____ INDEXED_____
SERIALIZED_____ FILED_____

SEP 20 1973
FBI—NEW YORK

b7C

b7C

224

FD-36 (Rev. 5-22-64)

23   F B I

                          Date: 9/21/73

Transmit the following in ___CODE___
                              (Type in plaintext or code)

Via ___TELETYPE___   ___NITEL___
                              (Priority)

- -

TO: DIRECTOR

FROM: NEW YORK (92-4564)

ELSUR, JOHN WINSTON ONO LENNON. BUDED: 9/24/73.

        REBUAIRTEL TO NEW YORK, 9/19/73.

        THE SPECIAL INDICES OF THE NYO AND CORRESPONDING RECORDS

WERE REVIEWED IN ACCORDANCE ~~░░░░~~ WITH CRIMINAL DIVISION MEMORANDUM

DATED 4/16/69, CONCERNING CAPTIONED INDIVIDUAL, WITH THE FOLLOWING

RESULTS:

        (A) NO.   ALL INFORMATION CONTAINED
                                HEREIN IS UNCLASSIFIED
        (B) NO.   DATE 5-2-83   BY 1678 RFP/Efm

        (C - F) NOT APPLICABLE.

        SUCH A REVIEW FAILED TO INDICATE THAT LENNON OR PREMISES

IN WHICH HE HAD PROPRIETARY INTEREST HAVE BEEN SUBJECTED TO ANY

LAWFUL ELECTRONIC SURVEILLANCE.

                                              92-4564-2652

1 - 92-4564 (SA ████ #53)   b7c
(1)   b7c

Approved: _John D. Malone_ Sent ____ M   Per ____
          Special Agent in Charge

                                              205

Then suddenly the Republicans pulled out, shifting their venue to Miami, for reasons never explained to this day. The effect was to undermine and weaken the protests, spurring even greater division and paranoia. A group called the Zippies was dogging Jerry Rubin and Abbie Hoffman with charges of selling out. Rennie Davis was being shunned by feminists. I was accused of burning buses when I wasn't even in town. Even the newly formed Vietnam Veterans Against the War (VVAW) was riddled with undercover agents. Inexplicably, however, FBI memos as late as June 1972 still warned that the Lennons were planning a huge rock concert outside the Republican convention hall. In July another FBI memo urged the Miami office that the Lennons be arrested on possession of narcotics charges during the Republican convention. They even fabricated a wanted flyer for Miami police with a photo purporting to be John Lennon saying "The Pope Smokes Dope" and describing him as "a former member of the Beatles Rock Music Group" (Wiener, 290).

Once the convention ended, however, the FBI folded up its mythic case, reporting in several memos that the Lennons had not been seen at all in Miami, quoting a source that the "subject" had "fallen out" with Davis, Rubin and Hoffman (August 30, 1972). The Lennon counterintelligence case was put on "pending inactive status" six days after the Republican convention and closed on December 8, 1972, one month after Nixon was re-elected (Wiener, 298).

No doubt British intelligence was after John Lennon in that year, not because of a token marijuana charge, but because he actively demonstrated against the British Army shootings of fourteen Irish civil rights demonstrators during "Bloody Sunday" in January 1972. Cable traffic revealed that Lennon had "offered entertainment" for the Derry cause, and intense efforts were devoted to monitoring links between American activists and the republican movement in Northern Ireland. One FBI document based on "information provided by a foreign government," presumably London, was totally blacked-out apparently because the discovery of a British spy operation could provoke "retaliation" toward the spymasters.

Having attempted to defame and neutralize this "former member of the Beatles Music Group," the FBI and government agencies fought fourteen years in court against disclosure of their covert campaign until 1992, when they were ordered to settle with plaintiff Jon Wiener and his ACLU lawyers. The following government officials and agencies were revealed to be in a single sinister loop to prevent an election-year concert tour featuring John Lennon: the president, the vice president, the secretary of state, the director of the Central Intelligence Agency, the director of the Defense Intelligence Agency, the Department of the Army, the Department of the Air Force, the Naval Investigative Service, the U.S. Secret Service, and the attorney general. (January 23, 1972, Memo from J. Edgar Hoover on "Protest Activity and Civil Disturbances," including [blacked-out] "Beatle singer John Lennon"; Wiener, 137).

In the end, some of the truth was revealed, but who was left to remember? Imagine what 1972 might have been with John Lennon on tour against Richard Nixon. Instead, the full weight of one, and presumably two, state spy agencies was brought down to fabricate charges, launch deportation proceedings and discreetly set in motion a plan to "neutralize" an artist they couldn't co-opt.

Asked in a *Rolling Stone* interview about "the effect on history" of the Beatles, Lennon perhaps foresaw the future:

> *The people who are in control and in power and the class system and the whole bourgeois scene is exactly the same, except that there's a lot of fag fuckin' middle-class kids with long hair walking around London in trendy clothes . . . but apart from that, nothing happened. We all dressed up. The same bastards are in control, the same people are running everything. It's exactly the same! They hyped the kids! We've grown up a little, all of us, and there has been a change and we are a bit freer and all that, but it's the same game. . . . The dream is over, it's just the same, only I'm thirty and a lot of people have got long hair, that's all.* (Jann Wenner, *Lennon Remembers*, Rolling Stone Press, 1971, p. 106)

There are many ways to remember John Lennon, of course. But we should always remember the John Lennon that the FBI and MI5 will do anything to make us forget.

Tom Hayden is an activist, professor at Occidental College, and a state senator in the California legislature. He was a leader of the student, civil rights and antiwar movements of the 1960s and 1970s, and the environmental, antinuclear and economic democracy movements from the 1970s to the present.

JIM HENKE

I NEVER MET JOHN LENNON, BUT TIME AND AGAIN OVER THE LAST FOUR DECADES HE HAS HAD AN IMPACT ON MY LIFE. THROUGH HIS MUSIC AND HIS LIFE, HE HAS SERVED AS A TRUE INSPIRATION AND HAS HELPED MAKE ME A better person.

I was ten years old when I was first introduced to John Lennon via the Beatles. The year was 1964, and like so many kids of my generation, I was captivated by the Beatles' invasion of America. I watched them on the *Ed Sullivan Show*. I bought all of their singles. But I had to be a little different. When all of the other kids were buying *Meet the Beatles*, I bought the green *My Bonnie* album by Tony Sheridan and the Beatles. Then I bought *Introducing the Beatles*. Of course, I eventually bought *Meet the Beatles*, as well as *The Beatles' Second Album, Something New, Beatles '65, Beatles VI* and every other recording they made. I went to see *A Hard Day's Night*. I bought Beatles trading cards, Beatles pins, Beatles magazines—everything and anything Beatles. They were like a breath of fresh air. It was like some whole new world had opened up to me.

Thanks to the Beatles, music became central to my life. I would sit up in my bedroom and listen to their music. Any time. All of the time. The Beatles set me off on a course that has caused me to spend virtually my entire professional life in jobs related to music.

At first, it was Paul McCartney who was my "favorite" Beatle. But as I got a little older and a little wiser, and as the Beatles began to mature as artists, I soon saw that it was John who was really speaking to me. Songs like "In My Life" and "Norwegian Wood" from *Rubber Soul* and "Tomorrow Never Knows" from *Revolver* showed me that a rock-and-roll song could be as potent as a great book.

As John's horizons widened, so did mine. Rock and roll had become my guiding light—and John was showing me the way. When he began his partnership with Yoko Ono, I, unlike a lot of other Beatles fans, was not bothered a bit. And as she encouraged him to speak out—particularly about the war in Vietnam—I followed in their footsteps. The fact that they were using their public position to take a stand on such an important issue truly impressed me. "Give Peace a Chance," the bed-ins, the War Is Over campaign—all of them left a mark on me. In fact, some thirty-odd years later, during the 2004 U.S. presidential election, I was utterly baffled when so many commentators criticized musicians and actors for speaking out and taking political stands. What was the problem? It seemed totally natural to me.

After the breakup of the Beatles, John's music continued to inspire me. The raw intensity of *Plastic Ono Band,* the beauty of "Imagine"—it was clear to me that John's solo work stood head and shoulders above that of the other Beatles. When John decided to take a break from the public eye in 1975, I, like many other fans, was disappointed. Yet, again, I admired his desire to go against the grain, to be a stay-at-home dad. At the time, that was almost unheard of—but now, of course, it is almost commonplace.

By the late 1970s I was working as a writer and editor at *Rolling Stone* magazine in New York City. I would occasionally see John and Yoko strolling on the streets of the Upper West Side, but I never had the courage to stop and say hi. I didn't want to be a pest. During that period, one of *Rolling Stone*'s columnists, Dave Marsh, wrote an open letter to John, urging him to come out of "retirement." Of course, in 1980, John did just that. It was a great moment, a moment that was shattered on December 8. I was in Los Angeles at the time, running *Rolling Stone*'s news bureau, and I was in my car, driving home from work, when

I heard the news on the radio. It was simply unbelievable that such a man could be taken from the earth in such a senseless, violent way.

Nearly twenty years later, in May 2000, I received a call from an associate of Yoko Ono's. By this time, I was the chief curator of the Rock and Roll Hall of Fame and Museum in Cleveland, Ohio. Yoko had been a big supporter of the museum since day one. She loaned a large collection of John's personal effects—his *Sgt. Pepper* uniform, some school report cards, a black leather jacket from the Beatles' Hamburg days and so on—prior to the museum's opening. And she came to Cleveland for the Hall of Fame's opening celebration in September 1995. But the year 2000, her associate pointed out, would mark two key anniversaries in the life of John Lennon—what would have been his sixtieth birthday on October 9 and the twentieth anniversary of his assassination on December 8. Yoko thought the time would be right for a major museum retrospective, and she wanted to do it at the Hall of Fame.

It didn't take me a second to say yes. My staff and I put all of our other projects on hold, and I flew to New York to meet Yoko at the Dakota. The things she showed me in that first visit floored me. I hadn't thought of John Lennon as being the kind of person who saved things, yet, there in the Dakota, Yoko had everything from school notebooks, report cards and various outfits from John's career to his drawings and handwritten manuscripts.

Over the next few months, I worked with Yoko to put this exhibition together. It was the largest exhibit devoted to a single artist that the Hall of Fame had ever undertaken, and, because of what John meant to me, it had to be great. It was a treat to work so closely with Yoko, and it was also a mind-blowing experience to be able to see so many of John's possessions up close. The lyric manuscripts, in particular, were astounding. There was "In My Life" written on the back of a large mailing envelope. There were the lyrics to "Lucy in the Sky with Diamonds," "Day Tripper" and, most astounding, "Imagine." I also loved the notebook in which a young John wrote a little newspaper that he called *The Daily Howl.* In it he showed his wit, humor and sarcasm, as well as his great artistic skills.

The exhibit truly opened a window into John's life. It was an experience unlike any other I had either before or after at the Hall of Fame. It opened in October 2000 and ran for nearly two years. I am happy to say that we were able to let hundreds of thousands of John's fans peek into this window. It was truly a memorable experience.

One of the most moving aspects of the exhibit were two items related to John's death: the blood-stained glasses he was wearing at the time, and the bag of clothing that he had been wearing that was returned to Yoko from Roosevelt Hospital. It was the most controversial part of the exhibit, both among the museum's staff and our visitors. Yet Yoko felt strongly that they should be a part of the exhibit, and she eventually wrote some text explaining that she wanted the world to see how tragic and senseless his death really was.

As a result of the exhibit, another opportunity arose for me. A book packager wanted to do a book that would include true-to-life reproductions of many of the items in the exhibit. Yoko loved the idea of sharing these items with people throughout the world, and she asked me to write the text. The book, *Lennon Legend,* came out in 2004, and it was yet another great experience, working with Yoko and learning more about John Lennon.

Between the exhibit and the book, much of my life the past few years has been devoted to John Lennon. And I have learned many things as a result. John showed me what an artist could be. He showed me what rock and roll could be. He showed me that you should stand up for what you believe in. He showed me about compassion. And he showed me how short, and tragic, life can be.

As I sit and write these words in the final month of 2004, I can't help but wish that John Lennon were still here. God knows, the world could certainly use him and his shining example right now.

Jim Henke is head curator of the Rock and Roll Hall of Fame and Museum in Cleveland, Ohio.

DENNIS HOPPER

ALL MY MEMORIES ARE IN THE MUSIC.

Dennis Hopper is a veteran actor whose films include *Easy Rider* and *Blue Velvet.*

Sir Mick Jagger

My first encounter with John Lennon gave me a sense of humility, which is funny in a way. I didn't know what to say to him. The Beatles were such a big deal then—this was in 1963, before we had made a record—and we weren't really anyone. We were just that one step away from being successful when they came to see us play. I mean, they were so huge. They weren't just musicians, they were like teen idols and larger than life. And they had *leather clothes,* which we couldn't afford yet.

One night when we were playing at a club in Richmond—we were only playing rhythm & blues and some Chuck Berry songs in those days—they came and stood in the audience on one side (wearing leather trench coats!), and I didn't want to look at them. I was too embarrassed. But John was really nice afterward. I said, "You play the harmonica, don't you?"—he'd played harmonica on "Love Me Do"—and he said, "But I can't really play like you guys, I just blow and suck. We can't really play the blues."

That was the first time I saw them. And they came to hear us play a number of times at the Crawdaddy and in the West End, and John came more often than the others. They used to hang around discos like the Ad Lib—this was around a year later (John used to like the nightclubs)—and I remember that one time, when we were all hanging out at one of the clubs, George was giving me a big spiel about how many records the Beatles had sold more than us. Which wasn't in dispute! He was so anxious to make the point. And after he'd heard all of this, John said, "Well, don't worry about George. He just hasn't got over the fact that he can sell records." He was nice about it. He wasn't always the caustic person he sometimes could be.

I liked him a lot. He was the one I really got on with the most. We weren't buddy-buddies but we were always friendly. But after the Beatles and the Stones stopped playing clubs, we didn't see each other that much. We were on tour and they were on tour. And, in a way, we were in competition in those days. Brian Jones, more than any of us, felt we were in competition—*everyone* was in *dire* competition then—and, if they were in America, we'd make a lot of capital about their not playing in England and all that. But we were friendly with them, I must say.

I didn't see John that much after that until he separated from Yoko, around 1974. We got really friendly again, more friendly than we'd ever been, in fact. We saw each other in L.A. a bit, but mostly in New York City and also out in Montauk, Long Island, where he came out to stay with me. We had some funny times. We got really drunk, and we went out on sailboats and just sat around with guitars and played. This was the time when John was preparing to record his rock & roll album, and he was quite openly trying to pick my brains, to decide what to record. We'd run through all the oldies, and he'd pick out ones that he liked.

And when he went back with Yoko, he went into hibernation. He was living close to where I was living in New York City, but I was probably considered one of the "bad influences," so I was never allowed to see him after that. On one or two occasions when I went to visit someone in the Dakota, I'd leave him a note saying: "I live next door. I know you don't want to see anyone, but if you do, please call." He never did.

I have in my passport a notation stating that the ineligibility of my visa is withdrawn "because of the Lennon precedent." He fought the court case concerning his visa problems because of his marijuana conviction in England—we were busted around the same time, actually—and he won it after five years and $250,000 worth of legal bills. So I have him in my memory every time I enter this country.

Sir Mick Jagger

There was one thing, though, about John: You were always a bit aware that he was "on." You felt relaxed, but on the other hand you weren't, 'cause if you let your guard down, if you said anything stupid, he'd jump right on it and take the piss out of you. I think all that fame and money made him a bit overguarded, first of all mentally and, at a later date, physically. But the Beatles had always had the feeling that they couldn't go out. They led a sheltered life; they never went out to the corner to buy their cigarette papers, for instance, and they used to comment on the fact that I did. At that period, of course, there were queues of girls outside one's door, and you couldn't go out. You had to send someone out to buy ice cream. But after a while that went away and one could live the life one normally leads, except that people would stop you on the street to say hello. But John was still living a sheltered life until he and Yoko moved to New York. And he thought he was much freer here. He walked out on the street, and people would say, "Hello, John," and that was it. He liked that, but I think—and this is the ironic and awful part of it—that he still felt that he wanted to stay protected from the outside world.

Sir Mick Jagger is lead singer and a founding member of Rock and Roll Hall of Famers the Rolling Stones.

GARLAND JEFFREYS

I WAS IN AND OUT OF THE RECORD PLANT IN THE EARLY 1970S. I HAD FOUND A HOME WITH A BUNCH OF GREAT PEOPLE COMMANDEERED BY ONE OF THE BEST RECORDING ENGINEERS OF ALL TIME, ROY CICALA. ROY WAS UNIQUE IN every way, in his recording techniques and his terrific sense of humor. He guided me, along with a brilliant team of musicians, through my first solo album, recorded in studio B. Dr. John, Bernard Purdie, Paul Griffin, Chuck Rainey, Winston Grennan, David Bromberg and the Persuasions. Studio B is where I met John Lennon. I entered the room and sat down at the console, which I'd become very familiar with. Roy introduced me, and John was immediately a quipster. No aloofness, no cool, no Beatle-ness—pretty much a regular guy. Yoko was there as well, and she was friendly and welcoming. John was enthusiastic, not quiet or brooding. Any time I was in a recording studio I always felt it was my playground even though the clock was ticking away the dollars, and John had the same schoolyard attitude. He was playful and very appealing.

Around this time I was thinking about recording "Help." I think it was a few days later that I ran into John on the tenth floor and mentioned that "Help" was a favorite of mine. Wouldn't you know it, like any songwriter, the mere mention that you might want to record one of their songs brought a package with the lead sheet to my small studio apartment in Gramercy Park. John had sent it off to me. I won't act cool about this; I was thrilled that he had it sent over.

We ran into each other a few more times, always at the Record Plant. I knew Roy was having the time of his life working with John, and I had enough sense to keep my distance and stay busy with my own work while I was there. The excitement of his being around and accessible was really fun. A few hellos and a couple of waves were enough for me. Some time had passed, and I was in Paris working on a few songs for a new recording. I was with my dear friend Antoine de Caunes, and after a night out carousing, we had just gotten to sleep at around eight in the morning when the telephone rang. It was the president of the Beatles fan club of France with the horrible news. John's sudden death was a shocker and hearing the news stunned me. An end to someone I looked forward to seeing again, to getting to know maybe, to discovering what he was up to through his music. An end to his great creative juice.

I was never really a great Beatles fan when the early craze hit. Those Beatle melodies and lyrics were too teenybopper for me, as I mistakenly thought back then. I was in love with Motown, Bob Dylan, Ray Charles and then the Rolling Stones. John Lennon fit right in with this group. His point of view cut right through. He spoke to me, and I believed him. He had an edge, which I was interested in. He was serious, and he reminded me of Dylan. And he made me laugh. I never did record "Help," but I'm thinking about it again.

There are so many great songs and performances. Two of my favorites are "Instant Karma" and "Come Together." The albums that I liked the most, and that still inspire are *Imagine* and *John Lennon/Plastic Ono Band*. Going back, it's *A Hard Day's Night* and the *White Album*. The solo recordings, the songs, the sound, the musicians and the production and the flux fiddlers and his passionate renditions. The venom, the gentleness, his vulnerability and honesty on all his songs has given me license. We are always looking for a few clues, some direction, a bit of information, a little style, some guidance, permission if you will, to take a few chances. It takes some courage and I'm always so excited when it's handed down to me. In 1980 I wrote "Jump Jump," and dedicated this song to John on my *Escape Artist* album in 1981.

Garland Jeffreys

JUMP JUMP

Let's make the great escape
All due respect to art for art sake
Jump Jump
We're gonna have some fun
For you and me and everyone

Jump Jump
To the rock and roll Rimbauds
Jump Jump
To the poets and verse
Jump Jump
To the Venus de Milo
Jump Jump
To the ones who came first

Garland Jeffreys is a Brooklyn-born author, singer and songwriter with lifelong ties to the New York City music scene.

Sir Elton John

John and I drifted into each other's lives for about two years. I was terrified of meeting him because of his biting wit and musical genius. But it was like meeting an old friend—he was warm, sweet and very funny. We played onstage together and we recorded together—two events in my career that I cherish.

But it was the man who impressed me most. He was so kind to my family, my band and my friends. There was *no* attitude, no swagger—just humility and warmth. It was as if for two years the sun shone directly on me and that heat has stayed with me forever. I loved him and will never forget.

Sir Elton John is an acclaimed singer/songwriter whose numerous awards include Kennedy Center Honors and Knight of the British Empire. A close friend of John Lennon, he cowrote the 1974 single "Whatever Gets You Through the Night."

LARRY KANE

THERE ARE SO MANY VIVID MEMORIES OF JOHN. AFTER ALL, I WITNESSED HIM AT SIXTY-TWO CONCERTS AND PRACTI-CALLY LIVED WITH HIM IN THE CONFINES OF AN AIRLINER AS THE ONLY AMERICAN REPORTER TO TRAVEL WITH THE Beatles to every stop on their 1964 and 1965 tours.

But when you assemble the memories of a relationship, the mind immediately and naturally moves to the one time that remains most meaningful, when a human being touched your heart as well as your mind.

John and I had something in common, the loss of a mother at a young age. John's birth mother died when he was fifteen, struck down by a car. My mother succumbed to a courageous battle against multiple sclerosis, just weeks before the great Beatles tour of North America in August 1964. She was just forty years old. I was twenty-one.

In the dimly lit late-night cabin of the Electra that transported us across America, a pensive and sometimes sad John Lennon joined me in commiserating over my mother's death. It was a bit of solace at a difficult time. In those years, John and I debated war and peace and many other subjects, but there was no disputing the fact that losing a mother was about the worst thing that can happen to you. In John's case his mother wasn't always there for him, so the permanence of her death was devastating.

There was one thing about John Lennon. In his steel-trap mind, he never forgot what was important to people. Fast forward to May 1975. I had become an anchorman in Philadelphia, and combined with a radio station, our TV station sponsored what was called the "Helping Hand Marathon," a weekend-long radio fund-raiser to benefit area charities, including the one most important to me, the battle against multiple sclerosis. With the help of our sales manager, Gene Vassall, I was able to put together a real coup—John Lennon to cohost the marathon for the weekend.

From the time I picked him up at the railroad station to his departure on Sunday night, John was sensitive, giving and tireless. On the phone days ahead of the event he said, "Larry, I know this is being done in memory of your mother. I will make this happen and it will be great, baby!"

It *was*. He even found time to do the weather on my newscast. It wasn't an accurate forecast, but who cared? John was in town meeting thousands of real people and leaving behind a legacy of unselfish giving that will always be etched in my mind.

Larry Kane is an Emmy Award—winning journalist who anchored the news for thirty-seven years in Philadelphia. His most famous assignment early in his career occurred in 1964 and 1965, when he was the only journalist to travel with the Beatles in their official party to every stop on their historic tours of North America.

ALICIA KEYS

I am a musician
I love music
It is my being
It is what defines me and it is ever changing as am I.
To me music is sacred,
Like a religion
I treat it with respect and integrity,
I learn from the musicians I love
The ones who care about what they play,
what they say
How the song can touch your core and shake your being
How the lyrics can make you weep
How the chords can change the world.
To me, that is John Lennon:
A musician who can touch the soul
One who cared about the world
A man who stood up!
A voice that simply sang to the part of us that needed to be spoken to
I thank God for a spirit that lives on through song and memory.
In the days of a drought, inspiration is hard to find
But with a man so diverse and passionate as Lennon
We will never be without a verse,

a prose,
a word,
a melody,
a chord,
or a song of which to grow from
I love my religion!

Alicia Keys is a Grammy Award–winning singer/songwriter/musician/producer/composer/author who has been writing and performing original material since age fourteen.

Astrid Kirchherr

Talking about the picture, it's a very close-up picture of John, and I took it in Hamburg when he was nineteen years old, and it was very, very soon after Stuart's death. Stuart was John's best friend, and

John always put on the macho type—you know, don't show any feelings—when he was young, but that picture does show all the emotions and sadness and loss he'd gone through in his then very short life, you know, the death of his mother and then the death of his best friend.

So that is why I really, really love that picture of him, because it shows the John I always wished he would be when he got older—you know, showing emotions so that you can see it in his face as well. I took it in the attic where Stuart used to paint in Hamburg.

Talking about John is very, very emotional for me because our friendship lasted only—well, it lasted forever, but we didn't have the chance to see one another later on when he was really grown-up and had a baby and was married to Yoko, so I can only talk about John when he was very, very young.

I've always admired him, and was very proud of the friendship we had together, and the first time John really showed his love for me was after Stuart's death, when he helped me such an awful lot to try and understand my loss—and his as well—and we used to talk about Stuart, and he really got me together again. He wasn't like Paul or George, who felt really sorry for me, and said, "Oh, everything will be fine." John just said—and I never forget that he said it to me one day when I was really, really down and didn't know what to do—he said, "Well, you have got to decide what you want: Do you want to live or do you want to die? Decide that, but be honest." And that helped me tremendously to go on. And then he said that there are so many things we haven't even discovered yet, and life has got to go on, and you can't sit down and cry all the time, you have got to get on, and if it's not for me, he said, it's for Stuart. And he said that in a very harsh voice, not like nice and sweet, but very directly, so that was the real John who was talking. And that made me really think twice about it. It helped me tremendously.

That is what I'm still thankful for, and to reminisce, to think about the old days when we were young and so full of hope, and just being anxious—what would the world have in store for us? And then knowing all he did when I never ever spoke to him—when he lived in America and did all this beautiful music—giving us "Imagine," that is so much for a man to do, to write and to think, and all I can say is I'm ever so proud to have met him and say he has been a friend of mine.

Well, that is about all, because John is still with me, and I'm still thinking about him, and to say the last few words: I'm so terribly proud of him.

Astrid Kirchherr is a photographer whose work in the early 1960s with the Beatles was both a key influence on their visual style and a significant catalyst to their career. She was engaged to Stuart Sutcliffe, an original member of the Beatles and John Lennon's best friend.

BILLY J. KRAMER

IN LIVERPOOL IN THE EARLY 1960S, DURING THE DAY I WAS WORKING FOR BRITISH RAIL. AT NIGHT, I WAS PERFORMING UNDER THE STAGE NAME BILLY KRAMER AT THE LOCAL ROCK VENUES. ON MANY OCCASIONS, I HAD THE HONOR OF being the opening act for the Beatles. In 1962 Brian Epstein offered me the opportunity to pack in my day job and have him as my manager. What a dream come true! At the same time, Brian was in the process of signing a group from Manchester called the Dakotas. Brian thought that they would be the ideal backing band for me, and had us all go down to the Cavern for a rehearsal, to see if the chemistry was right. To my surprise, John walked in and sat in the front row. That totally intimidated me, since even in 1962, I knew that he would change the course of rock-and-roll history. The Dakotas and I ran through a Rick Nelson song, and John proceeded to stand up and applaud and tell us how great it sounded. That was the beginning of a truly magical part of my life and a close working and personal relationship with John.

Shortly thereafter, Brian handed me a tape of a song that he wanted me to record. It was John singing "Do You Want to Know a Secret." At the end of the song, John apologized for the quality of the tape, as he had recorded it in the quietest place that he could find. With that, you could hear the flush of the toilet! That was an example of John's keen sense of humor. My recording of that song made me the first person to ever have a number one record with a Lennon-McCartney song. John later thanked me for believing in their songwriting abilities.

Soon after, both John and I were in Brian's office when John mentioned that he had a suggestion for me. John felt that if I added a "J" to my stage name and called myself Billy J. Kramer, that it would have a much better ring to it. How right he was!

Then Beatlemania happened! I was touring the U.K. with the Beatles and it was my twentieth birthday, when John came over to show me that they had entered the charts in the United States. Nobody was more deserving. He went on to say that he had written a great song for me as a birthday gift and that he would play it for me the next time I was recording at Abbey Road Studios. With all of the hysteria going on at the time, I was amazed that he actually did come to my session. He sat down at the piano and played "Bad to Me" and it was such a great song and I was thrilled. He then said that he would like to run another song by me to see what I thought. He proceeded to play "I Want to Hold Your Hand," at which point I said to him, "Can I have that one, too?" to which he replied, "Sorry, Billy, we're recording that ourselves next week." And of course, the rest is history!

What can I say except that I am eternally grateful to John for all that he did for me and for the rest of the world.

Billy J. Kramer is one of the original "British Invasion" performers of the early 1960s. Another Liverpool scenester, he was originally signed by Beatles manager Brian Epstein, and with his group the Dakotas notched several international hits on the Parlophone label with Lennon-McCartney compositions.

CHRISTINE LAVIN

I was in New York the night that John was killed. Like everybody else that night, I turned to a local radio station, WNEW with Vin Scelsa, and listened as everyone was calling in, crying and venting their outrage and sadness. It was a terrible tragedy, and that it happened in our neighborhood has always been a further source of sorrow. John loved the neighborhood, and we loved him, and people there were very respectful of him, and of his family and his privacy.

About eight or nine months after that terrible night I was coming home from a road trip. After a sleepless night of flying, I was in a taxi riding home from the airport when we crossed Central Park at 72nd Street and got stuck in morning rush-hour traffic right in front of the Dakota. As I sat there looking up at the Dakota, playing the sad events over in my head, John's song "Imagine" started playing on the taxi's radio. It stopped me cold, chills ran through me, and I started to cry. The moment I got home I sat down and started writing this song, "The Dakota."

THE DAKOTA

It was a Monday morning
I was coming in
from a long trip on the road

I flagged a cab near the East Side terminal
said, "please, take me home"
we drove up along Third Avenue
crossed through Central Park
when we came out at 72nd Street
I felt a cold chill in my heart
> Every time I see the Dakota
> I think about that night
> shots ringing out
> the angry shouts
> a man losing his life
> it's something
> we shouldn't dwell upon
> but it's something we shouldn't ignore
> too many good men have been cut down
> let's pray there won't be anymore

Rush-hour traffic was bottled up
we slowly inched by
I didn't want to look
but I couldn't help staring
at the scene of the crime
there was an old man
sweeping last night's dirt
out of the darkened vestibule
and a uniformed guard
in a gold trimmed cap
watching the world pass in review
> But every time I see the Dakota
> I think about that night
> shots ringing out
> the angry shouts
> a man losing his life
> it's something we shouldn't dwell upon
> but it's something we shouldn't ignore

too many good men have been cut down
let's pray there won't be anymore
 I don't believe in coincidence
 so why then on the radio
 did an old familiar voice
 echo back from not so long ago
 he said "imagine all the people
 living life in peace"
 well that's hard to do
 when you're on this
 blood-stained street
I wish I had the answer
to the simple question "why?"
I wish this taxi would go faster
I wish the driver would try
to leave this street
and leave this old building far behind
I wish I could take these bitter thoughts
and shake them from my mind
 because every time I see the Dakota
 I still think of that night
 shots ringing out
 the angry shouts
 a man losing his life
 it's something we shouldn't dwell upon
 but it's something we shouldn't ignore
 too many good men have been cut down
 let's pray there won't be anymore

Imagine all the people
 living life in peace . . .

Singer-songwriter, recording artist, and concert performer **Christine Lavin** has long lived in Manhattan's Upper West Side neighborhood, just a few blocks from the Dakota.

Annie Leibovitz

Annie Leibovitz's photographic work has appeared in *Rolling Stone, Vogue, Life, Esquire, Time, Newsweek,* and *Vanity Fair.* Her books include *American Music: Photographs, Women* (with text by Susan Sontag) and *Olympic Portraits.* Perhaps her most famous portrait is the 1980 photograph of John Lennon and Yoko Ono for *Rolling Stone,* which she took a few hours before John's death.

John LENNON 8012
w/yoko Ono.

Poet John   Donovan Leitch

I will write about my friend John Lennon, the poet and musician. But first, some history of John and my own upbringing to spice my memoir.

As children we both found ourselves growing up in British northern seaports, he in Liverpool, and I in Glasgow. Though I was three years younger than John, our background and exposure to traditional music and the Celtic literary past informed our eager young dreams to become working-class heroes. Lennon is an Irish name, and Dublin is just over the water from Liverpool, and the Irish families immigrated into the British ports, as they did into my own hometown. Like John, I am of Celtic descent, a race of poets and philosophers. This, and of course our love of Pop Music, brought us together.

John was the consummate Pop Music student. From the start he absorbed styles and performance skills easily and effectively. The deceptively simple lyrics of the popular songs of the 1940s and 1950s called John to emulate the writing and try his hand. When the R&B records came over with the sailors from America into the Liverpool record stores, John was amazed to hear what could be done.

Fast forward; he and I meet in 1965, introduced by the American poet Bob Dylan. I met the other members of the Beatles that night, and we all struck up a bond which served to protect us somewhat from the extraordinary fame and celebrity which had already begun to permanently alter our lives.

I would hang out with George, Paul and John and explore musical, social and spiritual interests. Visiting John's house I got to know him a little. We talked of the change we both felt could happen if we introduced certain ideas to the huge audiences we were attracting.

The work of the poet has always been to shine a bright light on the absurdities of society, challenging hypocrisy and greed and presenting the tools of change. At first resisted, poets' words herald a change to come.

And yet, serious thoughts aside, we were young and the music was our true deep love, the mistress who would lead us on into the groves of the goddess, and often we sang our new songs to each other, far into the night. I wanted to learn from John and he wished to learn from me. We were each other's fans. Recently, I was moved to hear that John had a secret jukebox, with his favorite artists' tracks—my own "Turquoise" song part of the box.

In 1968 we found ourselves playing acoustic to each other again, this time in an ashram in India. We both had been initiated by Yogi Maharishi and needed to know what Meditation could do for our suffering and that of the world. We had read all the books prior to meeting the Yogi, so we knew the intellectual truth, now we sought the experiential. Holy Plants had taken us part of the way yet left us wanting. We were there to meditate and explore the infinite; we felt like inner astronauts, diving deep within.

After the long sessions of sitting alone in our bungalows, we would meet on the rooves overlooking the Ganges and break out the guitars. And, oh, what a joy it was. For the first time since his first hit record, John was able to just strum for no one at all but himself. We had left the world of success behind, dropped out and boy did we need it. The media of the world had followed us to the ashram, camped outside the gates, but slowly they dispersed, leaving us to the privacy we were there to explore.

As it was only acoustic guitars we brought, I was naturally the one who played all day and night, acoustic guitar being my life. Paul and George also had their acoustics and we all strummed and wrote songs; they composed the songs which would become the *White Album* (I suggested this blank LP cover to John whilst in India). The *White Album* is strongly influenced by my acoustic styles and lyric descriptions. In particular, John's songs.

One day John chased a stray paparazzi photographer out of his garden; the guy had wanted to photograph John shampooing his hair. Oh, how we laughed to see John giving the guy hell and "effing and blinding" as he ran through the jungle. What a scene!

John returned to the garden, rinsed his hair and seriously said to me, "How do you do that?" John referred to the guitar style called "finger picking," he wanted to learn it.

I said, "It's called 'claw hammer' and has basic moves for four fingers on the right hand and 'hammer-on-off' moves for the fingers of the left chord hand."

John was unfazed and asked, "Will you teach me?"

I said sure and we began.

John took two days to get it and this is fast, as I took three days and nights when I first was shown the arcane secret by a tall Bohemian named Dirty Hugh. Hugh never washed and looked like Rasputin, but one must suffer for art, as they say.

Well John suffered a little over the lessons, but he was diligent, and when I said, "The frustrated brain has to be taught to relay the moves to the fingers," he said, "Fuck the brain, show me that again."

Slowly the magic pattern emerged, and the smile of accomplishment dawned on his face. Pleased with himself, as all guitarists are when they find a new chord and skill, John immediately began to compose in a whole new way. As the peacocks and elephants called across the jungle night, John's new songs could be heard tinkling through the dark foliage to my own bungalow.

The deep meditation stirred John's darkest and saddest heart, a song for his lost mother, "Julia." The sympathy for the reclusive young woman, who was in long, deep meditation for days to heal her pain, "Dear Prudence." These and other songs were growing from the new guitar style John had accomplished.

During the composition of "Julia," John asked me to help with the poem. I was flattered and a little wary as it was so personal to him. He was looking for lyric descriptions of a childhood he never had. Scenes of gentle beaches, with his little hand in his mother's, looking up into her "seashell eyes." These words are in John's song, but I can't remember if I wrote them or John. "Windy smile," another dream of his mother's joy, the lost memories he never lived.

I am filled with tenderness, and a tingle creeps up my back as I write, the spirit of John, the love I felt for my dear friend all those moons ago.

Our brief respite from our great fame and celebrity was over. Ending long weeks of peace and meditation, where we had refound for a little while the two boys we once were, free and unknown young poets of the goddess. As we parted after our stay in India, John gave me a gift of a drawing. It was of a girl with long black hair, her hand held over her mouth in a silent secret gesture. Around the circle of the frame John wrote,

"To Dear Donovan, see you in Merrie England, Scotland, Ireland or Wales." The girl in the sketch—was Yoko.

Donovan Leitch is a singer-songwriter whose hits include "Mellow Yellow" and "Season of the Witch." His autobiography, *The Hurdy Gurdy Man,* will be published in 2005.

JERRY LEE LEWIS

IT WAS IN ABOUT 1973 OR 1974 AND WE HAD BEEN PLAYING THE ROXY THEATRE IN LOS ANGELES. JOHN AND A COUPLE OF OTHER GUYS WERE SITTING UP IN THE BALCONY ABOVE US, AND I DON'T KNOW WHAT THEY WERE SMOKING, BUT MY sax player kept stretching up to try and sniff a little of it. Next thing I knew, John was on his knees in front of me kissin' my boots! When he stood up, he said, "Thanks, Killer, for showin' me how to rock 'n' roll." My son, Junior, was with me and started elbowing me. When John left, Junior said, "Daddy, do you know who that was?" I just laughed and said, "Yeah, Son, I know who that was."

Jerry Lee Lewis is a Rock and Roll Hall of Famer whose virtuoso keyboard skills and stylistic flair have influenced generations of musicians. His many hits include "Great Balls of Fire" and "Whole Lotta Shakin'."

Self-Portrait Was the Hardest MARK LEWISOHN

BY THE END OF 1969 I'D ALREADY DONE A YEAR, MORE, OF EXPLAINING JOHN LENNON AS BEST I COULD.

ABSOLUTELY THE BED-INS MADE SENSE.

BAGISM: MORE TRICKY, BUT COME ON—IT'S ALL FOR peace.*

Since John and Yoko had taped *Two Virgins,* their unceasing public doings had been his undoing. Lennon—and of course he was always "Lennon" in the British media—had alienated most of his fans, his public since the Beatles' explosion in 1963. And Lennon knew full well what was happening.

My mother was one such. And now here she was, telling a close

*Note from the editor. In an appearance on the *David Frost Show* on June 14, 1969, John Lennon explained this term. "What's Bagism? It's like . . . a tag for what we all do, we're all in a bag ya know, and we realized that we came from two bags, I was in this pop bag going round and round in my little clique, and she was in her little avant-garde clique going round and round, and you're in your little tele-clique and they're in their . . . ya know? And we all sort of come out and look at each other every now and then, but we don't communicate. And we all intellectualize about how there is no barrier between art, music, poetry . . . but we're still all—I'm a rock-and-roller, he's a poet . . . so we just came up with the word so you would ask us what bagism is, and we'd say We're all in a bag, baby!"

family friend about *Self Portrait,* John's latest "ridiculous idea" being to have made a film "showing his penis going hard." This being 1969, it was shocking to hear the word *penis* said in polite conversation. Especially by my mother. But before I could blush I began the defence, instinctively. I'm only sorry I've no idea what I said, but as I was eleven, I doubt it was wise or notable. I just remember being embarrassed and defiant.

I never did see *Self Portrait.* I really don't want to, though there is a kind of completist curiosity. To the best of my knowledge, though, it hasn't been shown since 1969, when Yoko allegedly said "the critics wouldn't touch it" and *Private Eye* magazine, inevitably, trotted out the standard schoolboy cock joke, "It won't stand up in court, officer."

Happy days.

Mark Lewisohn is a distinguished author and Beatles historian whose books include *The Beatles Recording Sessions* and *The Complete Beatles Chronicle.*

Michael Lindsay-Hogg

Glasses perched on a nose like a line drawing, smart and talented, unusual, sometimes tricky, really quick funny, spinning words like plates—all that, yes; but that wasn't the half of it.

Filtered early through Beatledom and later, sans Paul, even more clearly, he aimed, through Rock 'n' Roll and with his public persona, to acknowledge what it is we all share—vulnerability, occasional hubris, anger, temporary narcissism, wound, weakness, bravery; pushing to be better, to make himself better—through his songs, he was often his own most unflinching critic—more healthy, more able to talk about and deal with the vicissitudes we are all hit by.

The boy from Liverpool, abandoned by one parent and later, made bereft by the loss of another, in the first years of his fame, put on the guise of the cynic, someone who couldn't be touched inside. But his heart was pumping from an unassuageable hurt.

And then he met Yoko.

And she, through her art—"No, it's not like that, it's like this"—pushed him to seek what he always knew was there, his terra firma: total honesty (with a little bit of agitprop thrown in, like a chili in the stew) and a necessity to try to explain conflict and, in his telling of it, to understand it. And by conflict, I mean an admission of what it is we really do versus what it is we might wish to do, if only we could.

I always felt, when he and Yoko were doing their bed-ins and lie-ins, and when John grew his beard long, like an early ZZ Top, that as well as encouraging an alternative view, he was looking to escape the pop star identity that had been laid on him by the world-altering, and rightly so, success of the Fab Four. He knew that the kind of celebrity he had achieved had in it something of corruption; he distrusted it and felt it was in some way, in many ways, dangerous. "We're bigger than Jesus," and the records were stomped on and burned. And he chose, for a while, to put on the white face of a clown, because who would hurt a clown? Not that he ever ran from controversy, but he knew where unbridled-ness could lead. His humanity left him exposed, and his nature could not acquiesce to what was supposed to be.

Challenging and brave and, he was the first to say, imperfect, he gave us his nakedness and most of us were not able to give ours back. Too timid probably.

I am so glad I knew him. We both agreed that "Sh-Boom" by the Chords, which we would have heard, me in Ireland and him in England, on Radio Luxembourg in 1953 or 1954, was a really important record. I wish you would have had time with him, as I did.

Michael Lindsay-Hogg is a pioneering music video director who has worked with such luminaries as the Who, the Rolling Stones and Neil Young in his storied career. His work with the Beatles includes several short films and the 1970 documentary *Let It Be*. His stage and television credits include *Brideshead Revisited* and *Agnes of God*.

NILS LOFGREN

JOHN LENNON IS THE BEST FRIEND I NEVER MET. THE
BEATLES' MUSIC OPENED MY HEART AND SOUL AND TURNED
THE BLEAK, UNCERTAIN WORLD OF A CONFUSED YOUNG
TEENAGER INTO A BEAUTIFUL AND MEANINGFUL PLACE,
exploding with a rainbow of emotional colors, all radiating vast hopes,
dreams and inspiration through my human experience.

When John cried, "Help! I need somebody," I realized every mortal soul, regardless of our gifts, needs love, friendship and compassion from each other, and I was never again to feel quite so alone.

I stood in line at the record shop for every Beatles 45 single on release day. It never mattered if I'd heard the song yet; I knew I'd be inspired. I carried the 45 of "Don't Let Me Down" on my belt loop for months. I commandeered every turntable, anywhere, regardless of circumstance, and removed what was on to blast "Don't Let Me Down" through my psyche and the room. It was a lifeline I could never get enough of. No voice has ever touched or inspired me more.

John, thanks to the soul you shared, I'll never be let down again.

Nils Lofgren is a singer, songwriter, guitarist and guest member of Neil Young's band Crazy Horse. A much-sought-after studio musician, he also tours as a solo artist when not on the road with Bruce Springsteen's E Street Band.

NORMAN MAILER

WE HAVE LOST A GENIUS OF THE SPIRIT.

Norman Mailer is a journalist and author. In 1969 he received both the National Book Award and the Pulitzer Prize for *The Armies of the Night,* and again received the Pulitzer in 1980 for *The Executioner's Song.*

ALBERT MAYSLES

WHEN I THINK OF JOHN, A HEALING SERENITY ENGAGES ME AND ONCE MORE I'M SEEING HIM THROUGH MY CAMERA LENS AND ENJOYING WHAT I SEE.

IT WAS FEBRUARY 7, 1964, WHEN—CAMERA ON MY SHOULder and tape recorder slung over his shoulder—my brother and I met the Beatles as they arrived at the newly renamed JFK Airport in New York on their first visit to the USA. For the next six days we stuck with them, filming them day and night. I remember John as the most thoughtful, apparently taking it all in.

Albert Maysles is a documentary filmmaker whose projects include *Gimme Shelter* and *What's Happening! The Beatles in the U.S.A.*, a visual diary of their landmark 1964 tour.

PICTURES

JOHN'S LIFE WAS PLAYED OUT ON SUCH A VAST STAGE THAT PEOPLE TEND TO VIEW HIM IN PANORAMIC PROPORTIONS. BUT, I REMEMBER HIM IN SNAPSHOTS . . . HUNDREDS OF high-contrast, multidimensional pictures, some drenched in prismatic color, others in stark black-and-white. Some have begun to fade, others remain as sharp and focused as the day he became part of our lives.

I want to tell you about John beyond the veil of "entertainer" and bridge the distance between superstar and fan because much of his efforts were predicated upon this directive. When he referred to himself as a working-class hero, it was not metaphorical. He was the one who took the makeup off first. He was a nonshowbizzy guy. He spoke to you in a clear, intimate, truthful voice. At the time that was rare. That accounted for people thinking of his passing as a death in the family.

When people ask me "Who was the *real* John Lennon?" I always say, "You already know," because he never kept anything secret. He was real. He was exactly what was advertised, revered and sometimes scorned. He just put it out there. Nothing was censored or altered for mass consumption. It was a take-it-or-leave-it position. He wanted your attention, not your vote. He was an emotional provocateur. That was his charm. That was the beauty of the exchange.

We met in 1971; he ran out of time in 1980. The nine years shared with John were a gift. The thirty-five with Yoko remain a blessing.

GOOD NEWS AND BAD NEWS

I was a disc jockey in Los Angeles in 1971 and had interviewed hundreds of culture heroes of the times. The first day I met John and Yoko in person they gave me an acetate recording, *Sometime in New York City.* The record included such pop ditties as "Attica State," "Free Angela Davis," "The Pope Smokes Dope," "Woman Is the Nigger of the World" and a number of other really catchy tunes that would be immediately embraced by Clear Channel. In reality, it would get no airplay because, of course, nobody would touch it.

John, with much fanfare, handed me the acetate with no label on it. It had just come from the recording studio, and he said, "We've decided that you're going to be able to play the record first. You're going to break the record exclusively. We want you to take this back to L.A. and play it on the radio." To me, this was a great media opportunity; I was going to break a new John and Yoko album on the air.

I drove directly to the station but didn't have an acetate player in my car, so I never had the chance to hear it. I went back to the radio station and I played it, without commercial interruption, without intros or back announcements. I just said, "For the next hour, let's just all kick back and listen to something by John and Yoko. You've never heard it before. It's brand-new, and I'm fortunate enough to share it with you exclusively." In those days, on free-form FM radio you could do things like that without asking for permission.

The music resonated with me like "I Want to Hold Your Hand" resonated with the generation that preceded me, and the way "Thriller" did with the generation that followed. But even more than the music, even more than the record, was the purity and the innocence of these two people who would put it all on the line. The cover had a picture of Richard Nixon and Chairman Mao dancing together naked—Yoko felt that if that really took place, they would get to know each other better and we'd have a greater chance of peace in the world. Although the record certainly would not fly off the shelves at Kmart, for those who heard it and those who got it, the experience would impact their lives.

I can recall the expressions on the engineer's face through the glass of his brightly lit booth. I listened to the music through earphones. Undoubtedly, thoughts were racing through his head—Should we continue playing this? Will I lose my license for this frightening piece of propaganda? Should I lift the tone arm off the disk? He appeared to be shaken by it. That was the first public reaction. By the time we got to "Scumbag," I knew I better get the résumé out. The station did let me go, claiming they were "experimenting with their format."

I called John and Yoko. John asked, "How'd it go? How'd it go?" He was really excited. I said, "I've got good news, and I've got bad news. The good news is that I played it from start to finish without any commercial breaks." He said, "That's great! That's so f—ing great!" I heard him say to Yoko off the receiver, "He played it! He played the whole record! We got all the songs on the air! It's been on the radio!" I said, "As for the bad news, I may be looking for a new place to work." He thought that was hilarious, the funniest thing in the world, and he said, "Well, we're driving up to San Francisco, pack a bag and join the circus."

And I did.

JOHN

I always viewed him as a softy. That was the persona I found most engaging. If he were listening to us now, as Yoko is convinced he is, there would be a slight rumble at this point because he liked the idea of being thought of as a strong, assertive no-nonsense rocker. He was raised on Elvis, Carl Perkins, Jerry Lee Lewis, Little Richard . . . a band of gypsy musicians that took root in the 1950s and sprang to life ten years later. Of course, that was the pedigree. But there was so much more. I remember the first time I met him, how soft his hands were. I had interviewed lots of musicians because I was a disc jockey so I did a lot of handshaking—they had rough hands from playing guitar, calloused fingers, long nails to pull on the strings. But John's hands weren't working-men's hands. Those hands never used a shovel. If you look at photos of him in a T-shirt, he had what appeared to be muscleless arms. John was close to six feet but appeared smaller. He was delicate in his ways. He prepared tea carefully. He was fastidious and neat. He didn't like crumbs on the kitchen table or papers strewn about on a couch. There was a certain kind of civility in his interactions and in his speaking style when he did not have to deal with those who were seeking "Beatle John."

IN THE BEDROOM

John, Yoko and I spent a great deal of time—perhaps the majority of our time together—in their bedroom. The bed was made up of two antique church pews that were placed opposite each other with a piece of plywood between them and a queen-sized mattress placed on top. The bedding was simple and John slept soundly on a flat pillow. His dreams appeared in colors. John used to say they did their best work in bed. He was not being sardonic: they wrote in bed, they drew pictures, made their phone calls, he made his tape recordings, he had an acoustic guitar hanging above the bed that he would take down to play. That's where he watched his big-screen TV that he purchased in Tokyo—one of the first to be imported to the United States—so he could watch the news. That's where he kept his little "old English box" that contained stationery and pens and pencils, that's where he wrote his letters, answered fan mail, pasted collages, read his newspaper, listened to radio talk shows, smoked a little weed and where he would sometimes have his tea. It was a world within a larger world where he could watch the changing colors of the sky through the tall windows and be still.

There was a white wicker chair that leaned against the wall on Yoko's side of the bed. We would sit in that room and we would talk, debate, joke endlessly for hours at a time. We would begin at six in the evening. Yoko would doze off for an hour catnap. John would be on one side, I would be in the wicker chair, and when she grew bored with the boys debating something she had long ago realized, she closed her eyes and would go to sleep. John and I would continue, talking more softly. Our deepest and most meaningful exchanges took place in that room. Years before, Brian Epstein, the manager of the Beatles, was quoted as saying his favorite time was when just the five of them would be in a room together. For me, those countless hours in the wicker chair with John and Yoko were enough. Everything else was just dessert.

Occasionally we would put on our jackets. John would wrap a scarf around his neck, place a woolen hat or a familiar-looking cap on his head, adjust his glasses, and make sure the right boots fit with his nondesigner jeans. We would take the elevator in the Dakota building down to the street. Ten seconds after the gate opened it was another experience. It was the experience that fame had touched. He had gotten used to it, he would tell me. He was famous in Liverpool when he was sixteen. "It just got bigger," he used to say. The stage expanded. The audience grew. But he was always famous and dealt with the attention more seamlessly than all the others I ever observed.

FAME

According to the Associated Press they were, at that time, two of the most photographed people of the twentieth century. The kind of instant attention that surrounded them was overwhelming. Everybody knew John and Yoko. Of course, there were times when it was an intrusion. If he was having coffee with Yoko in a restaurant and somebody came by and asked for an autograph, they may not have been greeted pleasantly. But to have sixty people in your bedroom with boom mikes during your honeymoon, as they did during their famous bed-ins, that was doing the good work because they were "advertisements for peace." He just liked to choose the time and place, rather than have it chosen for him.

He would occasionally complain to me that, in the world of celebrity, nobody meets you in the present. Every person who approaches you is going to bring to the table something that occurred years before that was important *to them*. And it could be as mundane as where they were when "I saw you guys on the *Ed Sullivan Show*," to something far more obscure and more important to the person delivering the information, such as, "Don't you remember me? I picked up your scarf in Seattle just before you were going to get into your car when the fans were mobbing you and Ringo!"

He lamented the fact that because he would never meet anybody in the present, he was unable to develop new relationships. He was not permitted to contest his own silence. He was not allowed to sit alone and have a cup of tea, or walk down a beach, or stroll a street, or go into a record store without having to speak. The simple luxury of going through an entire day without having to talk to anyone or answer questions, was not an option. John could never be public and silent at the same time. Some people said he became a recluse and had lost touch with reality. Some people said he no longer appeared to be a populist or an advocate. I understand their point of view based upon media reports. In my experience with John, he did not go mad because he allowed himself to withdraw from "riding the merry-go-round." It was a choice that he exercised to assert his personal priorities. John and Yoko once placed a full-page ad in the *Los Angeles Times*. It was called "To those who ask, 'what, when and why?' " Yoko sent it to me with a check for $27,000 and said, "Just put this in explaining why we've decided to spend our time privately."

The great fear of all public figures is, If I withdraw will they forget me? John would occasionally express to me that maybe he really should be at Studio 54 with Mick and Bianca so he wouldn't be forgotten. Or he might pick up the *New York Times* bestseller list and be angered by the fact that he didn't see his name on it. When I said, "But you haven't written a book," he would say, "That's not the point." But those were fleeting thoughts. When John said he was starting over, it didn't take long before he was reminded that nobody would forget him anyway, as nobody ever has. He said to me, "If the work is good, it will always sustain you."

John also had the belief that you could utilize media as a spoken art form. Through interviews, he turned the power of the word into experiences that had not been tested before like "bed-ins," "bagism" and interviewing himself. Most of the time, these devices were not used to sell products. If you go through the entire body of his spoken word, most of it had to do with philosophical or political concepts, not because the record company said this is how you move product. In fact, after the Beatles broke up John Lennon never performed for pay. Every public appearance, every performance had to do with benefiting a charity or a cause. He took the money for making the records, he told me, because he viewed that as being something different.

YOKO

John loved Yoko more than anyone. I remember how he used to brush her hair . . . or when we'd be going out to a restaurant and she would put her coat on and he would adjust her collar so that it would look pretty and frame her face. Yoko was not a person who stared in the mirror, obsessed with clothing or her appearance. She never wore makeup. He was physically affectionate with her in private, and drew erotic sketches of her for public view. In their last video together, they removed all their clothes and tastefully hugged and kissed each other on a bed in a white room, two virgins sharing their love again for all to see.

He spoke through music in the first person. That's what "Help" was all about. That song was the first time that Yoko had ever heard the Beatles. She did not know that John had written it, but she had heard the scream. She was in Japan when she first heard it. That was John literally crying out for help. He told me that it was a time in his life when he was ashamed of the fact that he was over-weight, that he had been using pills, lamenting the absence of his father, a merchant seaman who left him as a child. In his own way, he felt that he was also somehow abandoned by his mother, though she was run down and killed by an off-duty police officer who was drunk at the time, while she was waiting for a bus. The live Beatles shows were becoming a circus. He couldn't see the audience. The audience could not hear the songs over the din of the screams, and they were on- and offstage in less than thirty minutes. He was just *screaming* out for help while lost in the abyss of spectacle. That's what Yoko heard and responded to. She was reading Kafka and exploring the "silent scream." Although they were yet to meet, she recognized his pain.

In the very early stages of our relationship, John told me that Yoko was the teacher and he was the student, and that there would be times when she will ask me to do things that will not seem to make sense. He said, "They don't always make sense to *me*, but I listen to her and trust her because she knows. Just go with it and wait until she disappoints you. If she does, then you can take issue with something that she says or asks you to do." He said that he was Carlos Castaneda and she was Don Juan. The sorceress. Yoko never said things like that. To her, they were simply the reincarnations of Elizabeth and Robert Browning.

John would make us laugh. He had a multilevel sense of humor—acerbic, understated, with an astounding talent for mimicry. For one of his birthdays, Yoko got him a complete collection of the BBC *Goon* shows. He sent me audiotapes he called "mind movies" which featured his various characters—the Great Wok, a Zen master named after a bowl in which people prepare rice and salads, Dr. Winston O'Boogie, Shingo O Yama, Sgt. Swade and an eccentric collection of others.

These characters had accents, vocabularies and points of view that made them seem like real people. Sometimes it must have been a relief not to be John Lennon. He could always make Yoko laugh. She seemed to enjoy the characters, but preferred John. She seldom brought him to that place where there was a punch line. He didn't look to her for laughter, he looked to her for comfort and wisdom. That's why he called her "Mother."

When people engaged in the endless public humiliation of Yoko in the media, nothing tee'd off John more. He said to me, "If she had blond hair instead of black hair, blue eyes instead of dark eyes, white skin instead of yellow skin, if she wasn't a feminist and a Jap, then they'd say she was beautiful." He tended to feel that most of the anti-Yoko press did not come down to people who simply did not like her music. He thought, "That's open season. It's fair that somebody did not wish to include her as part of their record collection. That's an individual creative choice." But with respect to the media invective, he felt it was primarily racist oriented.

In the 1960s, Yoko wrote an essay that appeared in the *New York Times* called "Woman Is the Nigger of the World." John was impressed by it, and he wrote a song with the same title and recorded it. He was singing about all women.

Woman is the nigger of the world
Yes she is . . . think about it
Woman is the nigger of the world
Think about it . . . do something about it

We make her paint her face and dance
If she won't be a slave, we say that she don't love us
If she's real, we say she's trying to be a man
While putting her down, we pretend that she's above us

Woman is the nigger of the world . . . yes she is
If you don't believe me, take a look at the one you're with
Woman is the slave of the slaves
Ah, yeah . . . better scream about it

We make her bear and raise our children
And then we leave her flat for being a fat old mother hen
We tell her home is the only place she should be
Then we complain that she's too unworldly to be our friend

Woman is the nigger of the world . . . yes she is
If you don't believe me, take a look at the one you're with
Woman is the slave to the slaves
Yeah . . . all right . . . hit it!

We insult her every day on TV
And wonder why she has no guts or confidence
When she's young we kill her will to be free
While telling her not to be so smart we put her down for being so dumb

Woman is the nigger of the world
Yes she is . . . if you don't believe me, take a look at the one you're with
Woman is the slave to the slaves
Yes she is . . . if you believe me, you better scream about it

We make her paint her face and dance
We make her paint her face and dance

Yoko put John in touch with his feminine side, made him confront his sexism in his art and in his life. She pointed out the one-sided messages in the early Beatle recordings and turned him on to the literature and the life of feminist perceptions.

John Lennon could have had his choice of an infinite number of women. It's not as if he would have trouble finding a date on a Saturday night, and of all the women on planet Earth, there was only one that became the eternal love of his life, and from the day that he met her until the day that time ran out, she was the one. For those who have this tremendous affection for John Lennon, they should keep in mind that the one that affected *him* the most was her. The one he loved above any other was Yoko. It wasn't as if there were four million Yoko Onos floating around planet Earth—there was one—and he was fortunate that she allowed him to be her other half. And continues to.

CLUB DAKOTA

We spent one New Year's Eve together in front of a giant Wurlitzer jukebox Elton John had given John as a Christmas present. It had been placed in a large empty room in an adjoining apartment that had just been recently acquired in the Dakota. John and I decorated the room for a special New Year's Eve experience. We explored some secondhand stores around Canal Street in downtown Manhattan and found some pink flamingo statues and an old couch that we brought back to the apartment. John wore his old Liverpudlian school tie, and we both got used black tuxedo jackets. He prepared an invitation for Yoko to join the two of us in this room at 11:00 PM and delivered it to her with a white gardenia, her favorite flower. He asked if she would dress for the occasion. She wore a gown. We waited until midnight. The snow was falling over Central Park and the blinking bubbles of the Wurlitzer moved through the glass tubes on either side of the giant speaker casting cascading multicolor lines and circles on the white walls. For the most part the box contained 1940s/1950s songs on either 78 or 45 rpm records. John greeted Yoko and the two of them danced together at midnight while I snapped Polaroid photos. It was the most romantic evening I shared with the two of them. Francis Ford Coppola could not have created an environment as exquisite. But the "Club Dakota" opened and closed after just one night. On a subsequent visit, I asked John what happened. He brushed aside the question.

THE LOST WEEKEND

When Yoko sent John to Los Angeles she basically said, "Go to Playboyland for all that stuff that you apparently seem to be missing." For a while, that seemed like a good idea to him. Then it became abysmal.

During the first weeks, there were a myriad of adventures:

Jerry Lee Lewis

By this time, I had become an entertainment reporter in Los Angeles for ABC TV *Eyewitness News*. On one occasion, I had the privilege of seeing Jerry Lee Lewis perform and interviewing him for television. John watched the interview on television. He had never seen Jerry Lee perform live. He had never seen any of his idols. That night, he called and said, "What do you think the chances are of me getting to see Jerry Lee?" I told John we could go to the Roxy the following night to see him perform. John asked if I would be able to introduce him to Jerry Lee. I assured him it would be no problem. "Okay, let's do it," he said.

I drove over to music impresario Lou Adler's house, picked up John and drove over to the Roxy. We waited in the parking lot until the security guy told us the lights were down. We went in the back door, moved along the side of the wall, climbed the stairs, and sat down in two seats high up in the balcony. Jerry did "Great Balls of Fire," "Whole Lotta Shakin'," "Memphis" and "Johnny B. Goode": he pounded on the piano with his shoes. He was inspired by the spirit of rock and roll and his body had become a host for that spirit. It's one thing to see a great performance, but this was church and John clearly felt the Holy Spirit. I glanced at him. He leaned over the balcony and there were times when he just was blissing out. Jerry Lee Lewis was one of the four or five people he had listened to as a child over the radio before he formed the Beatles. When it ended and Jerry was about to do his encore, I nudged John and said, "Okay, now before the house lights come on, follow me." I recall for a few unspoken moments he couldn't move. And he said, "Are you sure this is going to be okay? Does he know I'm here?" I said, "I don't think he's going to object to this at all. I really don't."

I didn't tell them that John was going to come backstage. During the encore, we went to the backstage area and waited. After Jerry came offstage and went into his dressing room, we waited outside his door for an appropriate amount of time before knocking. Jerry opened the door and said to me, "That was a nice thing, Son, that you ran on the news the other night, I sure liked that." "Thank you, Mr. Lewis," I replied. "I want you to meet a fan of yours. This is John Lennon. John, this is Jerry Lee Lewis."

John dropped to his knees and started kissing Jerry's cowboy boots. He was on his knees kissing those boots, not saying anything and not looking up. Jerry Lee looked down at him, put his hand on John's shoulder and said in a soft Southern drawl, "Now, now, Son, that ain't necessary at all."

Deep Throat

Around that time, *Deep Throat,* the first X-rated movie, had been released. John called one day and said he was curious to see it. It had been playing at the same theater on Wilshire Boulevard for more than a year—it was a cause célèbre. It involved many court rulings, it was pre-VCR, it was pre–Larry Flyntism and John wanted to see it. I asked whether I should try to get us in through the back door. John said, "No, no—you'd have to use my name to get us through the back door, which misses the point."

We decided I'd park across the street and John would wait in the car until he saw I had the tickets. Then he'd jump out of the car, and we'd walk in as the lights were going down. Of course, when we got there the closest parking was fourteen blocks away. So much for our plan. The movie was just such a big deal at the time, and obviously a big deal to John. So he decided to wait across the street and watch me as I got close to the box office. I stood in the line for about fifteen minutes, got our tickets and looked across the street to see about two hundred people surrounding John, asking for his autograph and wanting to know what he was doing on Wilshire Boulevard at 5:45 in the afternoon in front of an appliance store. He saw me as I raised my hand with the two tickets. Traffic stopped as he crossed the street and people in the line were reaching out to shake his hand. Cars screeched to a halt, horns starting honking, people rolled down their windows and yelled, "When are the Beatles getting back together again?"

It was immediately clear there were more people interested in him than in Linda Lovelace. He sat quietly in the packed movie theater. After twenty minutes in the darkness, he said it was time to go. To the best of my knowledge, pornography never played a significant role in his life.

The Red Light

During that time, I had four incoming lines to my house with different numbers. And because I have had insomnia since I was a teenager, my phones work on bells and lights. I had four different lights on the ceiling in different colors, so when the bells were off and someone was calling me, a green light indicated it was a friend, a yellow light indicated it was business, and a blue light was my answering service calling to say there was somebody who had something important to tell me. And there was a red light, or a hotline phone. That number was only known by John and Yoko. When I saw the red light blinking above my head while I was half-asleep, I would reach for the telephone and know that I would only be speaking to one of the two . . . sometimes both.

During those nine years, I must have spent a thousand hours on the phone with them. They called separately and collectively. On one occasion we spoke for twelve hours. The conversation started at noon and continued until midnight. I have never reported or revealed the contents of our conversations with anyone. When I had a girlfriend living with me, I would switch rooms before speaking. After a while, the girlfriends would switch boyfriends.

I told Yoko and John that during the lost weekend there would be no secrets kept from either of them. Yoko called every day; she just wanted to make sure he was okay. He called every day wanting to know when he could go back home. She would ask how he was doing, and I would say, "He has his good days and he has his bad days but the thing that he asks most is when can he come home." She said, "He's not ready yet." I would communicate that to him and sometimes he would accept it and sometimes he would say, "Call Mother and tell her I'm ready to come home." He had asked her on a number of occasions, "Can I come back?" and she continued to respond, "Not yet."

The red light blinked continuously regardless of the hour. It sometimes felt as if we were sharing the continuity of our lives through the wire. No subject was off-limits, many themes were recurrent. It was an electronic diary that predated e-mails by thirty years. I miss the sound of his voice. During all those years, they never changed their number.

Las Vegas

I was resting—I had left him at 5:00 in the morning, and he called at noon and said that he wanted to go to Las Vegas. He had never been there—could I pick him up somewhere—and I did.

From L.A., the flight to Vegas is just under an hour and flights left every hour of the day and he was ready, but first he wanted to have a drink on the way to the airport. There was a topless club called the Losers on La Cienega that Jim Morrison frequented. We went into the dimly lit bar where there were two or three dancers working an early shift. It was one of the first establishments of that kind around Beverly Hills, a fairly innocent kind of a show. John ordered a Brandy Alexander and put a couple of quarters in the jukebox. He watched one or two of the girls dance for fifteen or twenty minutes, then they came off the stage and wanted to know when the Beatles would get back together again.

"Let's get out of here," he said.

On the way out of the club he softly and half mockingly sang, "We make them paint their face and dance."

As we were driving away from there to the airport, he became very quiet. He had been up all night, and it appeared to me that the die had been cast. In a very brief period of time, he got a preview of coming attractions: he had left New York City, the woman he loved, his environment, the Dakota, the intellectual stimulation that Yoko brought to his life, his artistry, all the things that had meaning and value, and was now grabbing a quick one at the Losers Club, after being up all night drinking, and was on his way to Vegas. It was one of those moments where it was not necessary for him to speak to me.

There were a lot of those moments. John needed to shut down from time to time. I always honored his silence.

Las Vegas went by in kind of a blur; we weren't there for more than forty-eight hours. The snapshot I recall is this: We found ourselves walking through the casino like tourists. Late afternoon. John walked over and stared at a slot machine. He was just watching it, not playing, and a blackjack dealer asked me, "Is that John Lennon?" I said, "Yes. Yes, it is." "Is he just here having fun?" he asked. And I said, "Well, he's just here."

John asked me where the roulette table was and whether or not I had any money on me. He didn't. He never seemed to carry any. Of course, if he went over to the credit cage I'm sure they would have taken care of him, but it was easier to ask me. I told him I had about five hundred dollars. He said, "Let me show you how to win at roulette." That got my interest.

We went over to the roulette table and he said, "Just get one hundred." John didn't have a great familiarity with money. He would use phrases like "get me fifty" or "get me a hundred." I don't know if he knew if it was dollars or pounds or what it was because he never touched money: when he spent money, the money was invisible. Even years later, we'd go out to a restaurant with Yoko and he'd take out his American Express card. When it came to the matter of tipping, he would hand it to me and ask what the tip should be because he couldn't compute it. It was kind of like going to England for the very first time and getting out of a London cab and the driver telling you what you owe him and you've got this new currency in your pocket; it always seemed to me that whatever currency was in John's pocket was of a foreign nature to him and he didn't know what to do with it. And, like most well-to-do rock stars, he rarely paid for anything.

I was very interested in seeing what his plan was for winning at roulette, and I vaguely recall that he talked about playing in Hamburg, Germany. He bought one hundred one-dollar chips and said, "Watch this." With great aplomb, he placed a dollar chip on every single number except one. There are thirty-eight numbers on the wheel and John's theory was that if you put a bet down on every single number except one or two, when the wheel turned, the odds would be in your favor 97 or 98 percent of the time, so you would eventually win.

As soon as John reached the roulette table, the cocktail waitresses were there with Brandy Alexanders and Chardonnay. Thirty-five chips being piled up and shoved in your direction looks pretty impressive and one chip, of course, brings an impressive-looking return. After fifteen minutes he resembled Donald Trump, until one of the numbers that he didn't bet upon popped up and the dealer would clear the table of all the chips. Soon, he drew a huge crowd and the attendant madness: people were paying enormous attention, dropping hundreds on red or black and odd or even. Some bet with him or covered the numbers he did not play. Pit bosses appeared along with security people, while others wanted him to sign napkins. Word spread quickly throughout the casino. Dr. Thompson would have included the moment in *Fear and Loathing* if he had been present.

Needless to say, we lost all of my money extremely quickly.

THE END OF THE LOST WEEKEND

What was occurring in Los Angeles was a corruption of optimism, a real sense of loss over his separation from Yoko and a fear that he might spend an eternity being recalled as the guy who once played with the Beatles, and that terrified him. On more than one occasion, he said that the thought of appearing in Las Vegas with a piano or a guitar singing Beatles songs, regardless how much they paid him, would be an absolute horror and nightmare that he would never consider.

I have often wondered if he might feel differently about that subject today.

We were at a place called the Old World Restaurant on the corner of Sunset Boulevard and Larrabee. John liked the wooden floors and darkened alcoves, but on this specific occasion we sat outside on the patio. As we were sitting at a table watching the cars drive by, you couldn't help but smell the fumes. He was unshaven and somewhat unkempt, and appeared to anybody seeing him like a man on the skids. It was our breakfast hour after one of the Phil Spector *Rock 'n' Roll* recording sessions and John was eating scrambled eggs and pancakes. He was talking about Yoko and trying to devise new methods of convincing her to allow him to return.

As he was talking, a rather tall, exquisite-looking woman approached the table. She was wearing lots of silver bracelets, a tight black leather miniskirt and an emerald green Victorian-like blouse. "I don't want to disturb you," she said, "I just want you to have this. Use it when you're ready." She placed a napkin in his hand and walked away. He opened the napkin, glanced at it and handed it to me. It was a first name and a phone number.

He continued talking about Yoko and then we got in my car and drove back to Lou Adler's house. It had been a bittersweet evening: the adrenaline rush of those *Rock 'n' Roll* sessions was spirited and intense. Phil Spector created sounds that you could not shake. They stayed with you long after the recording sessions. Some of those masterpieces never go away. It was an emotional time, and there was a lot of alcohol and marijuana that accompanied John's reflections and experiences. I've never spoken about them in detail, and I am still reticent to start now. However, as I dropped him off and was preparing to leave the house, he asked if I still had the napkin. I did. "Call her," he said.

So I did. And the next day I drove over to pick him up to take him someplace and she was there in a robe, still wearing those bracelets. She said, "I remember you from yesterday at the Old World." I walked down the hallway and found John, and he said, "Get rid of her." I politely asked if she needed any vehicular transport to her destination. There was no need, she said. She would find a cab.

He was withdrawn for the rest of the day, and asked if I had spoken to Mother. It was the beginning of the end of the lost weekend for him because he recognized the obvious. He understood where it was going: he could spend a lifetime collecting phone numbers scribbled on pieces of paper. At age thirty-four, he knew that's how it might be forever. There would be a thousand amorous women in terry-cloth robes waiting around in the morning while he assigned someone the task to "get rid of her." He had already been there.

He had never been a bachelor. He married his first wife, Cynthia, because she became pregnant with his child and that was what a "real man" did in Liverpool at the time. He virtually abandoned his first son, Julian, to fulfill the destiny of being a Beatle, traveling the world. The local promoters and record company advance people would stock the hotel rooms with wall-to-wall groupies and women who were extremely accommodating and would not ask for autographs. There had been hundreds of them around the globe along with all the drugs and drink that the most famous musical group in the history of the world could ask for, without having to ask . . . and he seldom said no.

And finally he screamed out for help and was saved by Yoko. So, here he was again, reliving a time that had died years before. He just needed to be reminded of what was never there, and Yoko knew he would see it in time. It didn't take all that long. As soon as he glanced at his reflection and saw the past masquerading as the present, he realized that there could be no future without her and he had to get home.

Not long after that, he appeared at Madison Square Garden, walked onstage unannounced at an Elton John concert, sang three songs and made the building shake. It was his last public concert. After the show, he returned to his dressing room, and Yoko was there with a white gardenia. Ten months later, on October 9, 1975—John's birthday—Sean was born.

SEAN

I remember watching him place Sean over his right shoulder, stroking his back and the top of his head, while starting to whisper all of things the two of them did together that day as he was carrying Sean to his bed. He did this in the softest and most delicate of ways, not only in the way he whispered but in the delicacy and grace of his movements. I clearly remember his tonality and phrasing. By the time they reached the bed he would gently lay Sean down, and his words became increasingly hypnotic. It was his way of putting a baby to sleep instead of saying "get away from the television." It did not surprise me when I first heard the rough mix of *Double Fantasy* and the song "Beautiful Boy": *The monster's gone, he's on the run, and your daddy is here.*

All the things about househusbandry that others mocked were to John the most important and revolutionary thing he ever did. Raising a child came before all else. Now, it just so happens that Yoko has a head for business. Yoko came from a long lineage of Japanese bankers that could have put the Beatles to shame financially. But the concept of a man, a father, a husband, raising the child while the wife gets up in the morning and goes to work and brings home the bacon was unheard of. It was so radical; it could fall under the category of an anthropological Darwinian evolutionary reversal of roles. It was that potent. How many couples did that and spoke of the joys of the experience publicly? And the fact is that now, thirty years later, when it's become a little more commonplace, not a lot, but a little bit more, it tends to only slightly negate what a revolutionary act that was.

John delighted in the experience. And it was one of the reasons between 1975 and 1980 that he did not make public utterances and why he was not seen frequently and why he did not do a lot of interviews. It was time to raise Sean . . . time to play . . . time for Sean's feeding. There were times when I would phone and he would say, "Would you call me later? I'm about to bathe Sean."

John was raised by his aunt Mimi, and he wrote things down on scraps of paper or did crayon drawings or doodles. They may just have been scribbles on the backs of pieces of paper. At the time it didn't seem terribly important—he was a kid—and she innocently tossed most of them away. Years later, after he became a father, he would go on about things like that for *hours*. "Can you believe she would do that?!? Every single thing that Sean draws or touches, or if he makes a paint mark on a napkin, I save it, I keep it. It's Sean. It's a part of him."

Sean's recollections of his father, of course, are sketchy. It's a peculiar feeling when he occasionally asks me a specific question about his father, something he read, or heard. They shared only sixty months together. I understand for Sean, much of it must be somewhat of a blur. For John, it defined his life.

HOTEL OKURA

On one occasion, a courier appeared with a ticket for me. I traveled with them to Karuizawa, Japan, where we stayed at the Mampei Hotel, a magnificent, traditional place with a glorious ancient tradition, until the numerologist said it was time to leave. We were directed to Tokyo, where we stopped and remained in the Presidential Suite at the Hotel Okura for an extended stay. The suite was so large, John and I played soccer in the living room. For security reasons, you'd take the elevator from the lobby and with the right pass key it would go up and open into the living room of the suite.

One night John and I were just sitting in the room, I don't remember where Yoko or Sean was. We had ordered room service and may have had a drink or two. It was a dark, cavernous space, and silent. Outside one of the floor-to-ceiling windows was an exact replica of the Eiffel Tower—pre–Las Vegas—the Japanese liked that. We had just come from the ancient Mampei Hotel. It was complete culture shock returning to the "Western" part of the Eastern world.

Around ten o'clock that night, I was sitting on the couch and John was strumming his acoustic guitar. I was staring out at the Eiffel Tower and just lis-

FUJIYA HOTEL · ·MIYANOSHITA·HAKONE·JAPAN
JAPAN'S MOST DISTINGUISHED RESORT HOTEL

Dear Eliot,

It's not where you are
It's where you're at!
Shing Oyama
(representative).

love from all.
P.S. We only stayed 2 days!

FRONT VIEW, FUJIYA HOTEL

POST CARD

VIA AIR MAIL

Eliot Mintz
8522 OAK COURT
Los Angeles
California,
90046.
U.S.A.

♡ Yoko

tening to him play. He was a marvelous acoustic guitar player, even when he was just tinkering. Suddenly, the elevator door opened. I presumed Yoko had returned, but instead a middle-aged Japanese couple who neither of us had seen before walked down the hallway and entered the dimly lit room. They noticed that there was a man playing guitar and another man seated near a table. There were a few other chairs and tables in the spacious but modestly decorated room. The two of them looked around observing the tatami mats and expansively decorated shojis as well as the inexplicable presence of a soccer ball in a corner of the cavernous room. They spoke softly in Japanese, and seemed to want to listen to the solo music for a few minutes. I immediately understood what was happening. They were not waiting for Yoko. They had not been buzzed up. Somehow the elevator went to the wrong floor and they thought that they were in a restaurant or lounge on the top floor of the Hotel Okura.

After about ten or fifteen minutes passed, I noticed they were turning their heads awaiting some kind of server to ask if they wanted cocktails. I caught a glimpse of John who looked back at me with a grin that simply said, "Go with it, this is cool." He played the song "Jealous Guy" in English. It was beautiful, I loved it. After another five or so minutes, the Japanese couple, clearly dissatisfied with the service and not able to understand the musician, got up and left. And when the elevator door closed, John and I just rolled on the floor. It was the only time I think he ever performed for a private party of two.

They did not leave a tip.

CHRISTMAS WITH PAUL AND LINDA

When I went to New York, I always stayed at the Plaza Hotel. I stayed there for twenty-five years and never once slept over at the Dakota—I wanted to give them their sense of privacy. I still haven't slept one night at the Dakota. Sometimes, they would show up far too early in the morning for me. The phone would ring. "Hi! We're in the lobby and we're going to have split-pea soup in the Edwardian Room, can you come down here in ten minutes?" "I'm in my pajamas," I'd say and John would joke, "No problem, nobody will notice, you're sitting with John and Yoko." We would have our split-pea soup while gazing at the snow falling over Central Park beyond the huge glass windows of that timeless hotel. Often, we'd walk back to the Dakota through the park . . . a distance of about twenty blocks. We did so on one Christmas Day. I can't remember the year.

I thought it was just going to be John, Yoko and me. Then, Paul and Linda McCartney appeared. They obviously had been invited and John escorted them into the "white room," the living room, and the five of us sat there. Because it was Christmas, there was a branch of a pine tree, maybe two feet long, that sprouted from a vase that had been placed in the center of the room. That was the Christmas decoration.

Paul and Linda were charming. I didn't find the meeting or the conversation tense at all. Linda said, "Why don't we go up to Elaine's and have a Christmas meal together?" We did. The guests didn't see anything they liked on the menu, so Linda said that there was a great pizza place not far away. "Do you think Elaine would mind if we sent out for pizza?" Linda asked. I had the feeling that would be a social faux pas, but I also sensed that Elaine probably wouldn't ask the group to leave. The pizza was delivered, and we had our Christmas meal. We returned to the Dakota and sat for a while as the sun began to sink behind the downtown skyscrapers. The conversation became less rhythmic, the words more sparse. I was paying close attention to John and Paul and the way they looked at each other. It was a snapshot of two guys who altered the culture of the world forever through their words and music. But during this Christmas sunset, it was obvious to me that the two of them had run out of things to say to each other. After a while, Paul said something like, "I think it's time for us to go." Yoko would remain friends with Linda until the end of her life. Her last conversation with her was two weeks prior to Linda's passing. Yoko and Paul have yet to reach a comfort level with each other.

John spoke with Paul after that Christmas, but I don't know if Paul ever returned to the Dakota. It was interesting to see them together in that environment, but sometimes the things of one's youth just wane, after the sun has set a few too many times.

For the record, when I interviewed John for *Eyewitness News* during a walk on the beach in Malibu, he told me, "The wounds have all been healed."

THE END

During the last year of his life, John was just sailing. He was so affirmative and optimistic. He had a vision of the future. There was clearly a resurgence of the muse, and he spoke about his life with great enthusiasm. I would come to New York to attend the *Double Fantasy* sessions, and then we would take the tapes back to the Dakota, go up to the old bedroom late at night and he'd play the demo tracks of the songs with a beaming smile on his face. He knew what they had created.

In our private conversations, the Beatle he spoke of with the greatest degree of fondness was Ringo, and every tale he ever told me about him was filled with good humor and great recollections. Ringo held a dear place in his heart. After

John's death, the first phone call we received from any of them was from Ringo. I took the call. I was in the Dakota. He was calling from a pay phone outside of the airport and had just heard what happened. He said he and Barbara wished to be there. They were good with children and just wanted to come to the Dakota to be with Sean and comfort Yoko. Would I meet them a couple of blocks away and somehow walk them through the back gate, he asked. I did and have never forgotten their generosity of spirit.

YOU CAN'T GET A HANDLE ON LENNON

John not only made music, he used the interview format to paint word pictures. He wrote books, created drawings, lithographs, assembled collages, marched in the street, took out full-page ads, rented billboards, spoke out publicly about everything, made movies, created bed-ins, contributed generously to causes he believed in, sometimes behaved outrageously, defied convention, added an essential link to the chain of musical expression, advanced the concept of househusbandry, provoked dialog and debate . . . and commanded attention through revelation. It really didn't matter if you thought of him as saint or sinner, mediocre or brilliant, heroic or naïve, a working-class hero or an isolated dreamer . . . everybody had an opinion. He touched you.

That's why people see him in a panorama, because all this stuff went by in a forty-year life span, and we shared half that time with him. You can't get a handle on Lennon. Which could be the reason we're still talking about him and wondering what might have been. We're still trying to make sense of it all. We know where and when it began. We remember how it ended. But we will never know why. He embodied the best and most idealistic moments of our youth. Yet in some indefinable way each of us who cared about what he represented are confronted with the inevitable erosion of spirit that is emblematic of his absence.

I was blessed to have spent the time with him I did and wish you could have done the same. But if the truth be told, you were never that far away.

Elliot Mintz is a media advisor whose dozens of clients include some of the most well-known names in entertainment. Mintz's intimate friendship with John Lennon and Yoko Ono began in the early 1970s. His close relationship with the family endures to this day.

Letters to the Editor

A Love Letter From John And Yoko To People Who Ask Us What, When, And Why:

The past 10 years we noticed everything we wished came true in its own time, good or bad, one way or the other. We kept telling each other that one of these days we would have to get organized and wish for only good things. Then our baby arrived! We were overjoyed and at the same time felt very responsible. Now our wishes would also affect *him*. We felt it was time for us to stop discussing and do something about our wishing process: The Spring Cleaning of our minds! It was a lot of work. We kept finding things in those old closets in our minds that we wished we hadn't found. As we did our cleaning, we also started to notice many wrong things in our house: there was a shelf which should never have been there in the first place, a painting we grew to dislike, and there were the two dingy rooms, which became light and breezy when we broke the walls between them. We started to love the plants, which one of us originally thought were robbing the air from us! We began to enjoy the drum beat of the city which used to annoy us. We made a lot of mistakes and still do. In the past we spent a lot of energy in trying to get something. We thought we knew what we wanted, wondered why we didn't get it, only to find out that one or both of us didn't really want it. One day, we received a sudden rain of chocolates from people around the world. "Hey, what's this! We're not eating sugar stuff are we?" "Who's wishing it?" We both laughed. We discovered that when two of us wished in unison, it happened faster. As the Good Book says—Where two are gathered together—It's true. Two is plenty. A Newclear Seed.

More and more we are starting to wish and pray. The things we have tried to achieve in the past by flashing a V sign, we try now through wishing. We are not doing this because it is simpler. Wishing is more effective than waving flags. It works. It's like magic. Magic is simple. Magic is real. The secret of it is to know that it is simple and not kill it with an elaborate ritual which is a sign of insecurity. When somebody is angry with us, we draw a halo around his or her head in our minds. Does the person stop being angry then? Well, we don't know! We know, though, that when we draw a halo around a person, suddenly the person starts to look like an angel to us. This helps us to feel warm toward the person, reminds us that everyone has goodness inside, and that all people who come to us are angels in disguise, carrying messages and gifts to us from the Universe. Magic is logical. Try it sometime.

We still have a long way to go. It seems the more we get into cleaning, the faster the wishing and receiving process gets. The house is getting very comfortable now. Sean is beautiful. The plants are growing. The cats are purring. The town is shining, sun, rain, or snow. We live in a beautiful universe. We are thankful every day for the plentifulness of our life. This is not a euphemism. We understand that we, the city, the country, the earth are facing very hard times and there is panic in the air. Still the sun is shining and we are here together, and there is love between us, our city, the country, the earth. If two people like us can do what we are doing with our lives, any miracle is possible! It's true we can do with a few big miracles right now. The thing is to rec-

ognize them when they come to you and to be thankful. First they come in a small way, in everyday life, then they come in rivers, and in oceans. It's goin' to be alright! The future of the earth is up to all of us.

Many people are sending us vibes every day in letters, telegrams, taps on the gate, or just flowers and nice thoughts. We thank them all and appreciate them for respecting our quiet space, which we need. Thank you for all the love you send us. We feel it every day. We love you, too. We know you are concerned about us. That is nice. That's why you want to know what we are doing. That's why everybody is asking us What, When and Why. We understand. Well, this is what we've been doing. We hope that you have the same quiet space in your mind to make your own wishes come true.

If you think of us next time, remember, our silence is a silence of love and not of indifference. Remember, we are writing in the sky instead of on paper—that's our song. Lift your eyes and look up in the sky. There's our message. Lift your eyes again and look around you, and you will see that you are walking in the sky, which extends to the ground. We are all part of the sky, more so than of the ground. Remember, we love you.

John Lennon & Yoko Ono
New York City
May 27, 1979

P.S. We noticed that three angels were looking over our shoulders when we wrote this!

DESMOND MORRIS

THE FIRST THING YOU NOTICED ABOUT JOHN, WHEN CHAT-
TING TO HIM, WAS THAT HE ALMOST SANG AS HE SPOKE.
SOME SINGERS TALK IN A RATHER BORING VOICE AND THEN,
WHEN THEY OPEN THEIR MOUTHS TO SING, SOMETHING ODD
happens and a completely different sound comes out. This was not
the case with John. Even in casual conversation he seemed almost
incapable of losing that strangely yearning, gently strident tone of
voice that suffused all his compositions. And the way he put his words
together, taking a theme and gradually varying it, building on it and
letting it grow, made almost everything he said sound like the lyrics of
a song he had yet to write. To give an example, here is the verbatim
reply he gave to a question of mine when, in an interview in 1969
(when the Vietnam War was still raging), I asked him if he was optimistic about the future:

> I can't wait. I'm so glad to be around and it's going to be
> great and there'll be more and more of us and whatever
> you're thinking there, Mrs. Grundy of Birmingham-on-
> Toast, you don't stand a chance. You're not going to be
> there when we're running it, and you're going to like it

when you get less frightened of it, and it's going to be wonderful, and I believe it, and of course we all get depressed and down about it, and when I'm down and Yoko's down, Desmond will be up, or somebody else will be up. There's always somebody carrying the flag and beating the drum, so they—whoever they are—don't stand a chance, because they can't beat love, because all of those bits from religion about love being all-powerful are true, and that's the bit they can't handle.

I can't imagine anyone but John Lennon replying to my question in that way, with those speech patterns. I liked the way he spontaneously conjured up a Mrs. Grundy of Birmingham-on-Toast to represent all the gloomy pessimists. Although it is more than a third of a century since she fleetingly entered our conversation, her name has stuck in my memory and cannot be dislodged. That is the knack with words that John had. He sang so much that he simply couldn't stop the lyrics pouring from him even when there was no music.

My first encounter with John had been five years earlier, when he was celebrating the publication of his first book, a collection of surreal verse and prose called *In His Own Write.* My wife and I were invited to attend the Lennon launch party at Jonathan Cape in London. This was in April 1964, at the height of Beatlemania, when John was being mobbed everywhere he went, so that he had to be smuggled into the building to prevent a crowd forming outside.

It was a small gathering of editors, authors and critics, and we were all drinking and chatting noisily when, at last, John appeared in the doorway. If our guest of honor had been one of the world's greatest novelists, the babble of conversation would hardly have missed a beat, but John's sudden appearance brought an instant silence to the large room. With a wry smile he waved his arms and called out, "Carry on talking." There was some nervous laughter as the sophisticated literati realized that they had just been caught momentarily behaving like awestruck fans, and then the babble resumed. One of the authors had been bullied into bringing his teenage daughter with him. She remained struck dumb for much longer. Of course, if she had been that close to a Beatle at a pop concert in 1964, she would have been screaming, weeping, pulling at her hair and unknowingly synchronizing her menstrual cycle with the cycles of all those around her. Here, where she was the only teenage fan present, she did none of these things and simply fixated him with a disbelieving stare, as though he were a cartoon figure who had suddenly come to life.

John was at his most charming, bemused no doubt by the oddity of the gathering, which was so unlike anything he could have encountered in his usual professional environment. As a born rebel, he would have disliked most middle-aged gatherings of men in suits, but he knew that here, at his publisher's, the brains inside the suits were creative and probably just as rebellious, in their own way, as he was. So his slightly bored sense of duty in attending the party was tinged with respect and even a little apprehension.

He asked the father of the still-silent teenage girl about the Foyles Literary Luncheon that was due to take place the following week, and whether he would be required to make a speech. When he was told that, yes, he would be expected to entertain the august gathering with a short talk, he protested that he did not know what he could say. When it came to the day, he did, in fact, refuse to make a speech. He half-rose from his chair, said "Thank you and bless you" and sat down again, to everyone's dismay. Despite his rebellious spirit and the adulation that was being heaped upon him everywhere he went in the early 1960s, he had a genuine modesty about his literary ability, and, for a moment, his streetwise skills deserted him.

John was astonished by the reviews he received for his little book. Even the erudite *Times Literary Supplement* was impressed, comparing him favourably with Lewis Carroll and James Thurber, and announcing that the book "is worth the attention of anyone who fears for the impoverishment of the English language and British imagination. . . . Mr. Lennon . . . must write a great deal more." Mr. Lennon himself commented, "They took the book more seriously than I did myself. It just began as a laugh for me." But secretly, I suspect, he was delighted—he had broken out on his own, if only for a moment, explored new territory and had been rewarded for taking the risk. Only one critic voiced a sour note. When I was chatting with John at the launch party, the man, already well-wined and probably irked by the long wait for John's arrival, sauntered over toward us, beamed at John and said in a patronizing tone, "Congratulations on the book. It's great fun, but of course you have been so heavily influenced by Edward Lear." Without waiting for a reply, he plodded off to refill his glass. The implication was that John's work was hopelessly derivative, which was so unfair that I wondered how John would react. As the man's bulky figure disappeared across the room, John turned to me and said simply, "Who's Edward Lear?" I laughed, and we left it at that.

Privately, however, I was left puzzling over whether John really had never heard of Edward Lear's nonsense verse, or whether he simply meant, "Who cares about Edward Lear—I'm John Lennon?" I favoured the first explanation because, on the evening in question, John was being excessively courteous, modest and charming to everyone, working his way around the room like a seasoned, campaigning politician. It did not seem a context in which he might express himself arrogantly. Recently, however, I came across an essay in which the author reports that, as a young art student, Lennon "was intrigued by the nonsense verse of Edward Lear and the Goons . . . and subsequent notions of Surrealism and Dada. . . ." So perhaps I was wrong. Being patronized was something that John probably hated more than anything else. And his remark may have been more barbed than I realized at the time.

The older generation was, to his mind, a disaster area, and he had little respect for it. Authority was there to be ridiculed. Traditions were there to be broken. For example, in his book he created a character called Scruddy, a "working clog" who shouts at his superior, a "big fat catipalyst boss": "Why don't yer shut yer gob yer big fat get or I'll kick yer face in. Yer all the same you rich fat Bourgies. . . ." And it is easy to see this outburst as a reflection of John's early social attitudes.

Success created a special problem for him. The amazing Beatles steamroller flattened everything in its path. John was uncomfortable with much of it, but it was unstoppable. How can you rebel against a society that is feting you in every way imaginable? If he made a rude comment about polite society, everyone laughed and applauded the sharpness of his humour. His abrasive quick-wittedness in press interviews became legendary. For him, it was easy, because internally he still despised the establishment and found their fawning over him a further sign of how stupid they all were.

When George began to show an interest in the "Mystical East" and persuaded the whole group to pay a meditational visit to India to attend the Maharishi Mahesh Yogi, John went along for the ride, but privately was deeply skeptical. He enjoyed the surreal nature of the experience but soon became bored with it. And his native cunning told him that, as happened with the followers of all religious cults, they were being conned.

During a private conversation in 1969, I asked him how he had been able to stand all that Yogi nonsense, and he replied that every so often he would secretly slip away for a very hot curry. Not much of a rebellion, but it was apparently all he could manage at the time. I noticed that he did, however, put the boot in more effectively later on, when he wrote the lyrics to his famous "Imagine." There he deliberately encourages everyone to sing about how wonderful it will be when we realize that there is "no hell below us, above us only sky" and goes on to use the telling phrase "and no religion too."

A careful examination of the lyrics of "Imagine" tells us a great deal about Lennon's lifelong opposition to the hypocrisy of society. He had observed the way in which political and religious leaders, who were forever preaching peace and love, were in reality forever spawning war and hate, and the simple words of his song brought this home in an uncomfortable way. The lyrics attack nationalism ("Imagine there's no countries"), patriotism ("Nothing to kill or die for"), capitalism ("Imagine no possessions"), social inequality ("no need for greed or hunger"), religion ("Imagine there's no heaven") and the concept of the afterlife ("Imagine all the people living for today"). It is little wonder that a music-loving Russian, on hearing the song, announced that he was no longer a Leninist, but was now a Lennonist.

Peace protesters everywhere started to use "Imagine" as a kind of hymn, and the song's impact continued to grow and grow after John's murder in New York. Its message of universal love was attractive to many Christians, and the church appealed to John's widow, Yoko Ono, to allow them to omit the phrase "and no religion too." To her great credit she replied, "Of course it can't be deleted." Her wishes have not always been respected, however, the song sometimes being sung without the offending words. One poet even managed to recite her own version of the song using the phrase "and one religion too."

In 1969 I was approached by a television producer who was working on a programme about the most influential figures of the 1960s. The programme was to be called *Man of the Decade,* and the idea was that three people (Alistair Cooke, Mary McCarthy and myself) would each be given twenty minutes to make our respective cases. I was told that Cooke had chosen President Kennedy and that

McCarthy had gone for Ho Chi Minh. Who would I like to propose as the most important man of the decade? Like John, I hated anything to do with politics or politicians, and my first reaction was "the Beatles," who had brought so much pleasure to the 1960s. This was not permitted—it had to be just one man. Although it was unfair to the other Beatles, it had to be John, not just because I knew him, but because he was the rebel of the group.

In defence of my choice I explained that Kennedy and Ho Chi Minh had both been involved in a war that had killed countless young men, while John was a creative rebel who had given nothing but pleasure through his music. Furthermore, John was much more than just a pop star. He had introduced a whole new social attitude that had influenced his entire generation.

The key word was "irreverence." John's was not a glum, negative, insulting attack on society but a sharp-witted, entertaining, cock-a-snook approach that encouraged young people to express themselves as individuals and to reject the stifling rigidity of a lot of the older social traditions. Thanks to John, to give one example, regional dialects were no longer looked upon as a hindrance. He made no attempt to tone down his Liverpool accent (indeed, he exaggerated it) and this encouraged others to follow suit. Previously, without cut-glass Oxford English, it was impossible for anyone to make progress in the media. John changed all that, and a great deal more as well. So great was his social impact that there was talk of something called a "generation gap," in which the older generation was seen as antique and out of touch.

The television producer was delighted by my choice because of the variety it brought to his programme. My twenty-minute segment came last and, like the other two, opened with a personal statement defending the choice. This is what I said:

> *John Lennon, Man of the Decade. You may be shocked at the idea of setting up a Beatle alongside such men as Kennedy and Ho Chi Minh. I, too, find the comparison shocking, but for a special reason. It is the inheritors of the inspiration of Ho Chi Minh who, we are told, have buried their prisoners alive with their hands tied behind their backs. And it is the inheritors of Kennedy who, we are told, have shot down and massacred tiny children and old ladies. Yes, I am shocked by*

the comparisons. The Beatles certainly aren't in that league. They exploded into the sixties as nothing more than a source of immense pleasure and excitement for millions of young and some not-so-young people. But they then went on to become symbols of something more—symbols of a youthful irreverence and a lighthearted rejection of the growing staleness and hypocrisy of an increasingly materialistic culture.

The rebellion of youth in the 1960s is all too often measured in terms of brick-throwing extremists—the pathetic paradox of violent antiviolence—but this is too easy. It is a convenient but gross distortion of what has really been happening in the minds of the younger generation, and it has precious little to do with the great wave of exhilaration that started to spread as the Beatle phenomenon began to work its magic.

The message was simple enough: If you had talent and energy you could beat the system—you could have a ball—and to hell with traditional values and traditional symbols. The sixties was the decade . . . in which social foreground became more important than social background.

There followed clips from films about the Beatles and brief excerpts from a long interview I recorded with John in December 1969. I ended the programme by saying, "I am not suggesting that the rebellion of youth in the sixties, that I have symbolized in the shape of the Beatles, has arrived at any great solutions—it hasn't—but at least it has insisted on asking some vital questions, both pertinent and impertinent, and has rejected a great deal of yesterday's outworn dogma. And this is an important step that had to be taken. Let's hope that in the future we shall start to find some of the answers to the questions that youth has been so noisily and so rightly asking in the sixties."

I was sad that so little of John's long interview survived the editing process. Television is always wasteful in this way. Fortunately, however, a verbatim transcription was made of all of it, and I recently found what is probably the only surviving copy, among some of my old papers. Here are a few of the most interesting sections of it, much of which was never transmitted:

DM: John, the 1960s has been a time in which the attitudes of younger people have changed pretty dramatically, and you have been responsible for this change.

JL: I wouldn't take the responsibility. People used to say the Beatles changed the whole of Britain's image, or the Beatles were the leaders of the movement. It's true in a way, we were part of a movement—so am I—and the whole sixties bit, and the trip youth went through. The only thing I can compare it to is an acid trip. You start off with, say, rock and roll, and the late 1950s when all the kids, including me, were all James Dean and Elvis, and fairly paranoid and violent—that's what happens on acid, folks—then from there you start maturing, or thinking about the trip. The first effects of the drug wear off and you start coasting along a bit and you have time to look at the trees, and that developed into the actual acid scene, the psychedelic bit, and everybody goes grooving around with flowers and then, of course, like any drug, it wears off, and you're back to so-called reality, and the trip has changed you one way or another, but the basic nature is still there, and you might come out and be just the same as you were the first time, so a lot of the flower-power, let's-make-love bit developed into left-wing, let's kill them all, let's smash the establishment, but a lot of the residue still remains there and of course people tripped out again or started their trips at a different time, so we all went through this big trip and the violent rock-and-roll bit, then the love bit, and now we're out of it and making the decisions on what we'd learnt during the acid trip. Some people learnt nothing and some people discovered a new reality, and some people are still confident about the future, like we two are. Everybody's talking about the way it's going and the decadence and the rest of it, but nobody's really noticing all the good that came out of the last ten years—the Moratorium and the vast gathering of people at Woodstock—the biggest mass of people ever gathered together for anything other than war. Before, nobody had that big an army that didn't kill somebody, or have some kind of violent scene like the Romans or whatever, and even Beatle concerts were more violent than that, and that was just fifty thousand. So the good thing that came out was this vast peaceful movement....

DM: What do you feel, John, about the situation where you have a protest against something that you yourself are against, but the people take the protest to a point where it involves violence?

JL: Well, I think that's bad management. They start off with...a valid form of protest, but the establishment are like the school bully, and you either take no notice of the school bully or win him round, or slip him a soft one, or something, but you don't go up to him and shake your fist at him because he's going to beat you up. The school bully will always come up and pull your hair and tweak your nose until you react violently, and I think that's what happened to all the kids at Berkeley and the Grosvenor Square kind of fiascos. The bully—that's the establishment—they know how to beat people up, they know how to gas them, and they have the arms and equipment, and the mistake was made when the kids ended up playing their game of violence. And they know how to be violent, they've been running it on violence for two thousand years, and nobody can tell me that violence is the way after all that time. There must be another way, but a lot of people fell for it, and it's understandable in a way, because when the bullies are actually right there, it is pretty hard to turn the other cheek and run...to live and fight another day.

DM: The other question that I wanted to ask was this. You've been involved during the decade, firstly you might say in a purely musical statement and then later you started to explore other areas, and you explored meditation, and you explored the drug world as well. Those two phases in the decade, both for you personally and for a lot of other people, seem to be ending now. Could you make any comment looking back on those two phases and how that situation stands today for you?

JL: Well as for drugs and meditation, occasionally I'll meditate and perhaps occasionally I'll take some pot if somebody gives it to me, but it's not a big thing in my life. I'm on another kick now, which is brown rice, which does what meditation and drugs did for me with less hassle. I'm looking for an easy way out, the thing that I seem to have learnt from all this is that damn discipline comes into it somewhere, and I can't stand discipline, but it seems that whatever it is, even with drugs, you have to discipline yourself to get a benefit out of drugs, and you have to discipline yourself to meditate. All these things work, did what people told me, people say if you have acid you'll reveal things you've never seen. True. People say if you meditate you're more aware in the day. True, true, but I couldn't make that scene every morning. And if you eat brown rice, or a macrobiotic diet, you're in a higher state of awareness. It's like a permanent trip. True, true, but I still eat a bar of chocolate every three months, or whatever, and it's just like injecting a hard drug into you after you've been on a very pure diet, so I'm just still searching, as the papers put it. I mean, all these things work and do things, but whatever it is seems to be a drag or it seems like, whatever it is, discipline comes into it, and that's the hard bit.

DM: In this last decade people have stopped accepting things and started asking questions, and you've made a major contribution to this change. Could you comment on this?

JL: It's like the thing about starts with us, and when it started with me, George, Paul and Ringo and we said listen, man, there's another field of professionalism that doesn't need any qualifications except that you've got to get down to it, and want to do it, and you can make it in the terms of the world, the terms of reference they're talking about, you can make it without that pressure of the eleven-plus and GCE and all that, and everybody at the same time was finding that out, I mean I had my guitar, Mick Jagger had his in London, Eric Burdon was up in Newcastle, and we were all going through the same changes at once, and we all discovered that the values didn't mean a thing, and you could make it without college and education and all those things. It's nice to be able to read and write, but apart from that I never learnt anything worth a damn.

I have a vivid recall of the day of that interview—December 2, 1969. I was driving to John's house, Tittenhurst Park, from my home in Oxford, and on the way I heard, quite by chance, on the car radio, Cliff Richard attacking John for recording a song called, "Happiness Is a Warm Gun." Born-again Cliff voiced his outrage at a lyric that he felt might encourage violence in the young. When I mentioned this to John later, he thought Cliff's remarks were hilarious and replied, "It was meant to be satirical!" He went on to make some disparaging remark to the effect that you couldn't expect someone like Cliff to appreciate the use of satire in lyrics.

As I drew up outside the mansion, Yoko came forward to greet me with a kiss, and over her shoulder I noticed John's puzzled expression. I thought he quite looked put-out, and it occurred to me that Yoko may not have told him that she and I had a special bond. Two years earlier, before she had met John, Yoko had come to see me at the Institute of Contemporary Arts, where I was then the director. She was a struggling young artist who was finding it hard to generate interest in her work, and wanted my help, as head of the ICA, to arrange a screening of her latest avant-garde film, called simply *Yoko Ono No. 4*. Like all her work at the time it was totally outrageous, and few people would give it the time of day. But the ICA's brief had always been to encourage the most outrageous elements in modern art, and I promised to do my best to help her.

With difficulty, we arranged for the film to be shown at a public cinema in London's West End. When the audience discovered that *Yoko Ono No. 4* consisted solely of extreme close-ups of 365 pairs of naked buttocks, each pair being given fifteen seconds screen time, there was a near riot. Yoko had persuaded the owners of the buttocks to walk naked on a circular treadmill, and had filmed them one by one until she had enough for her film. The effect of staring at a long succession of these wobbling, undulating buttocks was strangely mesmeric.

By the time the thirty-sixth pair of buttocks appeared on the huge screen, one man could control himself no longer, leapt on the stage, and started caressing the giant buttock cleft that loomed above him. It was a memorable evening, and looking back on Yoko's 1960s' artwork it is now clear that she was about thirty years ahead of her time. The events, happenings and installations that she devised were puzzling to people when she first presented them, and by the time that such activities had become the mainstay of the modern art of the 1990s, she was largely overlooked as a serious artist. But, seen in retrospect, it is clear that she was historically important, having heralded the move away from the painted canvas toward the new kind of art that flourished at the end of the twentieth century. However, once she married John Lennon in 1969, her art was overshadowed by her new role as a "Beatle Wife." Even when she continued to present avant-garde events, such as "bag-ins" and bed-ins, they were now looked upon more as Beatle high jinks rather than as works of performance art. If she had not fallen in love with John, perhaps she would have gone on to become a major figure in the world of modern art. But her new image changed all that.

And here she was, freshly married to John and living with him in this grand house, standing in huge grounds that covered seventy acres. In the gardens near the house I noticed a crushed car wreck standing on a plinth as though it were an antique statue, and I made a mental note that Yoko's fertile imagination was still managing to find modes of expression.

Most of the long interview was filmed as we walked around the grounds. At one point I noticed some movement in a clump of bushes. On closer inspection it turned out to be another film crew. John explained that a BBC crew was filming us filming him. A few moments later a helicopter appeared and hovered overhead. "That'll be Japanese TV filming the BBC filming you filming me," John said—and to this day I do not know whether he was joking or not, such was the media interest in his every action.

Further days followed, as we worked out the details of the TV programme. There was one telling moment when we went together to select film clips at a viewing theatre in Soho. I was sitting several rows behind John and Yoko, and when the lights went down, they were silhouetted by the glare from the big screen. From where I was sitting I could detect that, as soon as they thought they were unseen, they started holding hands like young lovers. It had been said by some critics that a lot of their public canoodling was done for show, as if their love for one another was some sort of publicity stunt. Nothing could have been further from the truth. Their relationship was as intense as any I have observed.

Another myth was that Yoko had broken up the Beatles, but the truth was that they had started to break up from the moment that their manager Brian Epstein had died in 1967. As I mentioned earlier, John had never been entirely at ease with the wholesome mop-top image that Brian had created. He had no choice but to go along with it because of its whirlwind global success, but privately the rebel in him wanted something more. As the 1960s neared their end, it was John, not Yoko, who broke up the Beatles. It was he who insisted on having Yoko with him at all times, even in the recording studios, even though he knew the tensions this would cause within the group.

Yoko's appeal to John is obvious, when you consider his childhood. She combined the best qualities of John's mother, Julia, and his foster mother, Aunt Mimi. She had the wanton playfulness of Julia and the strict organizing drive of Mimi. (Significantly, John's nickname for Yoko, apparently, was "Mother.") Also, her sense of the surreal matched John's perfectly. And, as an avant-garde artist, she was strongly opposed to stale traditions and establishment institutions.

It was Yoko, John admitted, who had inspired his famous song "Imagine," and it was Yoko who encouraged him to play an active public role in opposing the Vietnam War. Although John was such a strong personality, he found himself enjoying the act of sitting back, for once, and watching the strength of this unusual woman impose itself on the world around them. He had reputedly slept with more than three hundred groupies in the Beatle years, but he had never found anyone with his special mixture of "surreal inventiveness" and distaste for authority. He had had a pleasant, delightful first wife, but Yoko offered him something more cerebrally challenging and more creatively stimulating. The two were about to set off on a journey of discovery together, a journey that would take them, not long after my *Man of the Decade* programme, to New York and a new life in the New World, one that, tragically, would eventually lead to John's murder one night, at the age of forty. It was a moment that made those of us who had known him feel a sharp pain of impotent anger. The only comfort was that his rich musical legacy was safe.

There remains the question of what it was that motivated John Lennon and drove him beyond ordinary fame to a level of achievement that sets him apart from and above most other composers and performers of popular music. It is rare that one gets the opportunity to ask this specific question of the person concerned, but in John's case I was able to do so, as part of the long interview that I recorded with him. This is how I worded my question and how he framed his reply:

> **DM:** What is it that drives you on? What is the thing that makes you keep going and keep expanding, because you're always going into new areas?

> **JL:** It's partly your ego I suppose, that drive, whatever it is, it's that intuition—you get ten ideas and one turns you on a bit, so to get the satisfaction out of it—if the idea's a great letter to a relative, the idea will excite you. I tended a bit in the old days to just have the idea and not bother to write the letter, but I've found that through the relationship with Yoko, and through the way that she works, she had a similar experience in a different field. I only followed through songwriting, or certain very specific things, but it's just the follow-through, you've had the idea, you've got to write the letter, and then you've got to seal the envelope send it to the person, then you get a reply and that is the turn-on. The applause for your creativity is the reply from that person, because the letter excited them or annoyed them, or whatever it is that the idea was. I can't think in terms of these hip drug thoughts—"you get the fix." I never fix. You get the buzz from creating. You get the milder buzz from the idea and then putting it on paper, or on record, or on film, or whatever the medium, in this discipline bit because I tend to think "Oh, couldn't the cameraman do it," or let's go away or something, but if you do it and then you get the reply, then that's it, that's the buzz, and then you get that "what's next" . . . it's like throwing a stone in the water and the initial splash is very exciting, but when the ripples come it's great.

The significant point that John himself makes here is that his principal driving force comes, not from the act of creation or its performance, but from the feedback that is obtained following that performance. He says "you get a reply and that is the turn-on" and, again, "when the ripples come it's great." In other words, what drove John was the need to be appreciated. When his mother dumped him on her sister when he was only five years old, following his father's departure from his life, he must have felt deeply unappreciated. And it would seem to have been our good luck that he spent the rest of his life trying to make up for this. His desperate need to convince himself that he was, after all, worthy of appreciation, was apparently what drove him on and on and on. The fact that his work was so often tinged with mockery, sarcastic humour, cynicism and light-hearted irreverence was testimony to the deep distrust he had of those who admired him. If he sucked up to them, he could not trust their responses. He had to test them to the limit. If, despite his famously acerbic wit, they still came back for more, then, perhaps, after all, he was worth something. He once said of his mother, Julia, "She had me, but I never had her." He wanted much more from his public and it was this that drove him on to fortune, fame, idolization and eventually, beyond fame.

There is the final contradiction of how a rebellious young tearaway ended up as an international campaigner for peace. To understand this transformation one only has to consider John's inner conflict. Here was an angry young man with a sarcastic disrespect for authority, who also had a sensitive, generous side to his complex personality. As a confused child feeling rejected by his parents, he had been shown endless care and protection by his beloved Aunt Mimi. As an adult this contrast left him yearning for the peace and love that he knew existed, but which, inside him, was always stifled by the distrust and pessimism from which he could not free himself. Incapable of finding an internal, personal peace of mind, he sought it elsewhere. But the truth is that, although his famous pacifist anthem "Give Peace a Chance" was ostensibly an impersonal plea to a warring world, in reality it was also a private cry to the turbulent demons inside himself.

Desmond Morris is a distinguished anthropologist and sociologist whose writings have influenced generations worldwide. In 1969 he interviewed John Lennon and Yoko Ono shortly before naming Lennon his choice for "Man of the Decade."

"Cousin Brucie" Morrow

John was "Beatle-silent" (he became a house daddy) for several years. We kept in touch, and one day, I decided to ask my fave-rave Beatle if he would like to step out of his home and bask in the sunshine of the Sheep Meadow in Central Park. I was about to produce and host a stage show for WABC Radio New York City and for the Police Athletic Club of New York. John said, "Coozin," (he pronounced "cousin" that way and I loved it), "I'd like to come but I will not perform. I would to say hello to you and my New York friends." I thought about it for nearly one second and told John it was a deal. I booked Alice Cooper, Johnny Maestro and the Brooklyn Bridge and a few other local groups to perform. John called me a few hours later and asked if he could bring a friend of his to join him onstage—Harry Nilsson would also like to say hello. Another no-brainer for me.

The day finally arrived after a major promotional campaign. It was a picture-perfect spring day in New York City. More than one hundred thousand people jammed into Central Park's Sheep Meadow to see John and the show. The audience was pumped and electrified—after all, this was John's first public appearance in quite some time. My friend John, the poet, star and activist looked out at the ocean of audience and walked over to me. He looked tense and nervous. I remember thinking to myself, "Can you imagine John Lennon having stage fright?"

"Coozin, there are so many people out there, don't they realize that I am not going to sing?"

"Cousin John, they all know that you're not going to perform, they just want to share space with you. They want to know that you are on the planet with them." John looked suspiciously back at me and asked if I was quite sure. It always amazed me that this poet, this humanitarian never realized his magic, that his friends and fans just wanted to be with a very special person.

I will never forget John.

"Cousin Brucie" Morrow is a New York City–based disc jockey who has been on the air more than forty years. He first met John Lennon on the Beatles' 1964 U.S. tour.

BOBBY MULLER

THE TWO MAJOR MOVEMENTS OF THE 1960S, CIVIL RIGHTS AND THE PEACE MOVEMENT, GAVE CAUSE TO A GENERATION TO PROTEST THE SOCIAL ORDER OF THE TIMES AND THE VALUES THAT SUPPORTED RACISM AND MILITARISM. THAT generation is referred to as the counterculture generation. If there was any one symbol of that generation it was rock and roll. The most influential rocker of the era was John Lennon, an icon in his own lifetime who found a voice beyond music and helped to inspire the politics of a generation, a country and the world. He was a leader in ways he never intended and became bigger than he ever imagined.

The Beatles were not in any way known as a political group. But Lennon broke from that group silence in 1967 when he publicly denounced the war in Vietnam over the strenuous objections of then manager Brian Epstein. From then on, there was no turning back. As much as Lennon rejected political ideologies, he was nonetheless a firmly committed anti-authoritarian who formed alliances and in many ways supported various justice movements. He was, however, best known for his peace efforts.

His song "Give Peace a Chance"—written and first performed on the last night of his Montreal bed-in in 1969—was sung days later in

Washington by Pete Seeger along with more than half a million protesters and immediately became the anthem of the peace movement. A couple of years later his political evolution to a more confrontational mind-set was revealed in the legendary "Power to the People." That year, 1971, also produced my personal favorite, "Happy Xmas (War Is Over)." That year he moved to New York City to be closer to the counterculture and antiwar movements that were making plans to more directly participate in the politics of the time. When it was reported that Lennon wanted to use his celebrity status to help galvanize a national concert series in 1972 and mobilize the newly enfranchised eighteen-year-olds to vote in opposition to Nixon and his war agenda, the powers-that-be struck back.

Senator Strom Thurmond wrote a secret memo to Nixon urging that the newly arrived singer/activist be deported. Sure enough, three weeks later the Immigration and Naturalization Service tried to deport Lennon. Nixon also ordered then FBI director J. Edgar Hoover to monitor and harass Lennon. (All this was revealed many years later in unsealed documents as a result of Freedom of Information requests.) In 1975, when the INS chief counsel resigned, he was quoted as saying the persecution of Lennon was more vigorous than the efforts to deport Nazi war criminals. Lennon had to fight for years to stay in this country, finally receiving his green card in 1976.

John Lennon added more than songs to the political movements of his times. He inspired people with his talks, his antics, his commitment, his networking and his major donations to various counterculture, justice-based causes. He was courageous in breaking free of the business constraints initially wrapped around the success of the Beatles. He withstood pressures from the authorities and willingly withstood severe public criticisms to hold true to his beliefs. His poet's vision, translated into the most memorable and inspirational songs of an era, is but a part of the legacy of this remarkable figure. I was proud, as president of Vietnam Veterans of America, to call on America to fly our country's flag at half-mast on the announcement of his tragic death.

Bobby Muller is founder and chairman of the Vietnam Veterans of America Foundation, which was awarded the 1997 Nobel Peace Prize for its efforts to ban landmines.

ANDY NEWMARK

I MET JOHN FOR THE FIRST TIME WHILE TOURING WITH GEORGE HARRISON IN 1974. I HAD DONE SOME RECORDS FOR GEORGE THEN. WE TOURED AMERICA, AND JOHN CAME TO ONE OR TWO OF THE SHOWS WITH YOKO AND SAID hello. So we shook hands, but had no real contact or communication other than just meeting each other.

Where the story really begins for me is July 1980 . . . about a month before the *Double Fantasy* sessions. I got a phone call when I was on tour in Italy with Roxy Music from Jack Douglas's office. Jack was producing *Double Fantasy*—could I do the dates? I was really happy and excited about the call. Fortunately, the Roxy tour ended two weeks before the *Double Fantasy* dates were going to begin. I immediately accepted over the phone. This was a really, really big deal for me because I grew up with the Beatles. I was thirteen years old when I saw them on *Ed Sullivan* so this was big. For some people, it's Elvis; for others, it's Sinatra. The Beatles are it for me, so this call was to die for.

I, along with two other drummers who were all working in New York at the time, had been recommended. They put the first call out to Steve Gadd. Steve never called them back. I've always said, "Steve redefined the meaning of the word 'busy' when you're so busy you don't even call John Lennon's office back to say 'No, thank you.' " Anyhow, I guess I was second on the list so I got lucky.

The job came to me and I was completely jazzed out of my mind that I was going to do this. I finished the tour in Italy with Roxy Music, and I then went back to Bermuda to visit my family. I thought I'd have two weeks to chill out before the session started in New York. I got there and discovered through the grapevine that John was in Bermuda! Yoko had decided he needed a spiritual journey like when she shipped him off to Los Angeles for the Lost Weekend. It was her idea, I think, that he should sail to Bermuda. I didn't contact him while he was there, but we talked about his trip once I got to New York and we were in the recording studio. He said he sailed to Bermuda on a fifty-foot boat. I asked, "Well, are you a sailor?" He said, "No, it was dreadful. Everybody was vomiting their brains out for the entire trip and even the dog on the boat was sick and the skipper and everybody . . . it was just awful." I was thinking, Gosh didn't anyone warn him? I had done that trip—it can be really terrible and you want to commit suicide when you're that seasick. I couldn't believe that someone had put him on this boat and set him off on this five-day trip. I was surprised he had the balls to actually do it.

John's trip to Bermuda was one of the first things we found as common ground to talk about. The first day I met him, he told me how much he loved Bermuda. He had not been home to the U.K. for a number of years because of his immigration problems. He said, "I had no idea somewhere so close to America was so English. . . . It was so amazing feeling as close as I could get to home and it made me realize I'm starting to miss England a lot." Because Bermuda is still a crown colony, he really connected with the English influences. Driving on the left . . . bobby policemen. He really liked it.

Shortly after his boat had arrived, his son Sean and his assistant, Fred, flew down, and they rented a little house. Every afternoon, John would go up to the Botanical Gardens, just outside of Hamilton. The English sense of gardening is very powerful in Bermuda, and the English do great gardens—it's one of their eccentricities. In Bermuda, the cosmetics of the place—everything is beautiful—all the houses and gardens are kept up very well amid ten- and fifteen-acre botanical gardens. He would go to the gardens every day with Sean, and they would walk around for a few hours, all through the flowers, and different trees . . . in the botanical garden, every tree and plant has a little black plaque with white writing imprinted on it that has the English name of the plant under the Latin name. In his walk through the gardens, he stumbled upon the name of a plant called Double Fantasy. When we were in the recording studio, he told me that the name just struck him and that it was going to be the name of the album.

For the *Double Fantasy* sessions, it was all really well-known session guys from the past twenty-five years who had big credits. Hugh McCracken, myself, Tony Levin on bass, George Small on piano, Arthur Jenkins on percussion and Paul Flick—all people we knew and respected.

We were all very aware that John had not been in the studio making music for five years. He had this self-imposed exile to get off of all the drugs, and to be a father and hang with Sean, and be all that he was not to his son Julian, and just try to be sober. All of us knew the old crowd that made his previous records: Klaus Voormann, Jim Keltner . . . it was an L.A. crowd and Jack Douglas had never done any work with any of the Beatles or any individual solo records or anything. This was a new producer, a new studio, new players, a new engineer—not part of the crowd John had been running with for many, many years. I asked Jack Douglas why we were there. He said, "Because frankly, John loves all those guys but they were so stoned and fucked-up, and there was so much drinking and drugs." John felt in his sobriety that he just didn't want to have those triggers and see those people, because it reminded him of something he was trying to move away from. As players, the people he had been associated with were amazing. Apparently this was the reason he and Yoko decided to get away from the memories and the guys, God bless them all, which he had gotten completely out of his head getting high with. So, we got lucky.

The first day began. We were all there. John was not there yet, but the players were all there a bit early and we were all visibly nervous. We knew each other. We clearly were nervous because we didn't know what to expect. Though it wasn't voiced, we admitted this to each other afterward. We weren't sure if he was really going to be on top of his game or not.

We were just sort of wondering how much compensating might we possibly have to do to help get this whole process of making music going again. Who was this guy and what was he going to be like sober? We were just edgy. Of course it was not out of humanity, it's because it was John Lennon. We obviously wanted things to go well because we were all completely buzzed to be there.

He arrived. When he walked in he seemed totally feet-on-the-ground. He was completely together, he was tan, his hair was pulled back, his eyes were crystal clear. His vibration was that of someone totally confident, grounded—someone who had his shit together. He just seemed totally at ease, full of humor, relaxed. He looked amazing. He looked healthy. There wasn't an ounce of fat on him, he was all skin and bones, but just really, really healthy-looking.

He wasn't making any excuses, like "Well, guys, I haven't been doing this for five years." He was ready for action.

Everyone picked up on that. We were wondering, "Who's going to take the helm?" John, Jack, the engineer? Where was the voice of authority going to be coming from? It's something you wonder as a studio musician that's part of the chemistry that goes on in the studio. You quickly discover who is real quality-control and who isn't. We weren't sure. So we got started and we started playing a song quite soon—he wasn't into fucking around—he was like "Okay guys, here's a tune, let's start playing."

We were playing and everything was a little tentative. I think he sensed that we were a little nervous and put his guitar down and said "Okay, right. Guys, I'm going to go in the control room and hear what you're doing and talk to you individually and get this thing up and running." In that moment he completely asserted his authority. He went into the control room. He said, "Right, guys. Count the tune off. Play."

We started playing the track. He stopped us right away. "Okay, Drummer"—he didn't even remember our names—"I'll get your name eventually." He was really blunt like that, but it was totally not offensive. It was just honest. He continued, "Okay, Drummer. One at a time now. What are you playing there in the verse of that song?" I'd play it. "Right, okay," he said. "Don't do that, do this." And he'd mouth out a little drumbeat the way he wanted the foot to go, or the snare drum or he'd sing the beat, you know, musician talk.

He said, "Okay, that's for you. Right. Bass player: What are you doing?" Tony would reply. John said, "Okay look. This is what you do. You don't do that, you don't do that, but you can go with those notes and those notes, but keep it like this. . . ."

He immediately focused us exactly where he wanted it to be. We weren't fishing. We weren't guessing. He immediately put us on a track, each of us on our own instrument, speaking to us in our own language. "This is what I want." And we got it. Whatever it was he said, we individually got it, and understood exactly what he meant. In twenty minutes, the whole thing was together.

He put us all at ease by demonstrating that five years out of the studio was not going to be a problem, that he was clear and focused and knew exactly what he wanted, and that he was clearly going to be the producer of this record, even though Jack Douglas was listed as the producer. But Jack was there for a number of reasons. He was someone to bounce ideas off of. John clearly had the vision of what this record was going to be. Jack was there to help John achieve that vision, but in the first thirty minutes we realized that it was going to be John who was calling the shots.

There was a chemistry in the studio, and we could get where he wanted to go quickly. The "Drummer" and "Bass Player" name thing went on for about five days before he started remembering our names. And he would say to me, "Listen, play like Ringo." And I loved it. I totally loved it. And I got it, because I knew all about Ringo and the Beatles, and I understood Ringo's vibe as a drummer. When I would get elaborate he would say, "Forget all that fancy shit. Play like Ringo."

John would say, "I want this to be done in three takes. I don't want to sing this all afternoon." He was singing live. A lot of the vocals he sang while we were recording the tracks were kept as final vocals. He only patched up where there were mistakes. He kept massive chunks of the guide vocal that he would do when we recorded the track. That was unheard of because technology allowed you to record the track and even though the singer might sing along while you were doing it, he would go back two weeks later alone in the studio when the musicians were gone and just do the vocals and sing everything again. John was singing guide vocals, but he wanted to keep those vocals. He didn't want to go in and doctor them. It takes a really, really good singer to be together enough to have your guide vocals be the final stuff. To do that premeditatively as an artist means you have an immense level of control over what you do. He'd say, "I only want to sing this song a few times. It feels great—there isn't any reason why we shouldn't have this. . . ." He wanted live performance, which meant, from the players' point of view, don't fuck around, don't get fancy, don't be self-indulgent, play something you know is going to work and that you can execute properly, immediately, because the artist in this case wants a finished product soon.

This approach focused us into playing minimal, but going with the feeling and supporting the song. He got the result he wanted. All the tracks on the *Double Fantasy* record we got in three or four takes. He inspired us, and we took heed of his words.

He wanted it to happen quickly and not turn into the self-indulgent recording process that rock and roll got into with people taking a year to make a record, and all that nonsense. And he had the talent to deliver and sing it and play it. We were made to feel that we better be on our toes. He was going for it. He brought the best out in us.

He was very clear with us on another matter: "Do not take Yoko's music any less seriously than you are taking my music, gentlemen." He not only said it, he conveyed it. It was very beautiful what he did. He did a song. We'd get the track, and he'd say, "Okay guys, now we're gonna do one of Yoko's." When Yoko's song came about he would put his instrument down and go into the control room and really produce the song and the track, which he was great at doing.

It worked. We'd do a song of Yoko's, then John would go back and we'd do a John song, then he'd put his guitar down and go back in and say, "Right, sweetheart, back in the studio." It was very loving and democratic the way he shared the bill with her, and never once pulled rank as John Lennon. He would call her "Mother." I have since adopted that, and oftentimes call Jan "Mom." Because relationships become indistinguishable in their roles between sister, mother, lover. As you get older you realize that nurturing takes on maternal, sister, brother aspects. John did it first, but I got it. They were tight. They had something. She was important to him.

Andy Newmark is a renowned versatile drummer who has worked with artists ranging from Sly and the Family Stone to Roxy Music. He appears on John Lennon and Yoko Ono's 1980 release, *Double Fantasy*.

PHILIP NORMAN

I SHOULD TELL YOU WHEN I FIRST MET JOHN, THEN HOW
OUR PATHS CROSSED AGAIN, AND THEN HOW I CAME TO
WRITE A BOOK, *SHOUT*, AND HOW I THOUGHT OUR PATHS
WOULD CROSS AGAIN, BUT THEY DID NOT, BUT THEN HOW
Yoko asked me over, a few months after his death, and I sort of saw
where he had been, but I missed him by those months. . . .

I first met John Lennon in 1966. That was when the Beatles were
on their very last British tour, when nobody realized at the time it was
going to be their last. I was working on a newspaper in the very north-
east of England, in Newcastle-on-Tyne, and I rather rashly said, "I will
try and get to see the Beatles and interview them." I waited at the
stage door of what was called the City Hall, in Newcastle, a civic
building, and sure enough a big limo drove up and out came the
Beatles. I'd still had a picture in my head of John as wearing a suit
with a round collar but he got out wearing a white T-shirt with something on it—T-shirts with messages and slogans were not very usual
in 1966—and as he passed the group of press people, including me,
he made a joke and shouted out something at us, sort of mocking, and
I thought, oh God, this is not going to be easy.

However, I got into the basement where they were and went in to interview them. I was allowed to go in, Paul McCartney took me in, actually. I tagged along with him when he came back along the corridor, and to my utter amazement, he and John and Ringo talked to me and I was so completely taken aback at how friendly, how easy to talk to they were, particularly John. Even then I realized that he must have done this a lot before, he made you feel as though you were the only person he'd ever really answered questions from, and sat on the arm of a chair, I remember, and Paul was there, he was very nice. I asked, can I stay a bit longer, and he said, yeah, sure you can, but of course a roadie came in and threw me out.

That was the last time I ever thought I'd see John Lennon. Then when I was working on the *Sunday Times* in the late 1960s, this color magazine was a very fashionable publication at that time, I was asked to go down to the Apple House, the Beatles' business, and just write about what was happening, because a lot of rumors had come out about what was happening, or what might not be happening—were they breaking up? were they losing all their money?—what was happening, really? They'd announced this new era of being businessmen, but John at the same time was off on this new tangent of performance arts with Yoko, whom he'd not long since met—would they be flying off in different directions at the same time? Supposedly they were now four businessmen running this enterprise that was meant to be a new kind of business which didn't have boring "men in suits" running it, as John always called them.

Derek Taylor, in the press office—an amazing character in his own right—allowed me to hang around the Apple House for several weeks. So I spent quite a lot of time hanging around this place—amazing access, extraordinary access, I still really can't believe it—including a morning in the room on the ground floor where John and Yoko conducted their peace campaign. Relays of all kinds of people were brought in to see them, and I was allowed to sit there and just watch the people come in and out. I remember Yoko was wearing a shift dress, it was purple and looked like tissue paper. John was chain-smoking and they had one of the robots in the Plastic Ono Band in the fireplace. A couple of young women from Texas were brought in—they were blind, and John and Yoko led them in so they could touch the robots in the Plastic Ono Band.

So again, I thought, this is amazing, this is the last time I'm going to see John Lennon. But a few days later, there was a party in the basement for one of the

Apple groups that became Badfinger. John and Yoko weren't there, but just as I left toward the end of the party, I suddenly met him in the doorway, and I—this is only a very small thing, it may not mean much, really—except that he just nodded "hello," as if he knew me. I always remember his nod, as if there was some sort of slight history, like he thought I was worth nodding hello to.

But it never occurred to me then that I would write a book about the Beatles because too many people seemed to be writing about the Beatles, turning out millions and millions of words every year, and it literally was a bandwagon, and there was no room for me on this bandwagon at all. But, at the end of the 1970s, I was talking to some colleagues from the *Sunday Times* discussing which subject for a biography would come up with the most immediate, huge readership and I said, "It's the Beatles." Of course by that time, in the 1970s, the Beatles' day was thought to be over. They had made wonderful music, but they were bracketed "in the 1960s." I was told by my colleagues, "No, no, you're wrong, everybody knows everything there is to know about the Beatles; there's nothing new to say." I thought that there was, and if one looked there would be something to say, so I started doing some research. It meant going through John Lennon's life from the very beginning, meeting his Aunt Mimi, meeting boys he was at school with. I went through all of their lives, but John's just had the most fascination. I suppose because I identified more with him—broken home, drawing and cartooning, that kind of thing—I came to know so much about him.

The Beatles—all of the ex-Beatles at this point—were in a state we now call denial (we didn't have that useful term at the end of the 1970s) but it had been such a terrific shock to their system being the Beatles that they just all wanted to get away from it. John in particular wanted to get away from the whole music business. I'd heard one or two people say that he was looking after his son Sean, and in fact his aunt Mimi gave me his address and I wrote. I got a polite letter back from one of John and Yoko's assistants, saying, "Thanks for your interest, but not at the moment." But I thought that it would still happen, I just had a feeling that if I wrote again and maybe again, I would be able to go and see him. Soon after, the *Double Fantasy* album came out and he returned to the public domain and seemed to be very relaxed and at peace with everything. I thought this really is a good chance, before I hand my book to the publisher, I'll be able to talk to him. That didn't happen. The tragedy of his death happened one night when I had just delivered my manuscript to the publisher, with the proviso that I hoped I would add something about John Lennon from him personally.

It was just this awful moment when people still held out some hope that the Beatles might get back together. John very robustly resisted this idea—he said that they'd be rusty and out of practice and it wouldn't be worth it. The UN secretary-general pleaded with them at one point in the late 1970s to do a reunion concert. After John's death, people realized it was the real end of the Beatles. His death was an awful tragedy—it was unlike anything else. I suppose you could only compare it with the death of Kennedy, because there was no sense that the people were over-reacting, there was no sense that people were showing too much emotion. Everybody was absolutely heartbroken.

My book had to go into production without having the hoped-for word from John. When I finally came to New York to publicize the book, *Shout*, in 1982, I was on a television program and talked about John. Yoko saw me and phoned me and said she'd liked what I'd said about him and asked if I'd like to come over to the apartment in the Dakota. I finally did get to visit his home in New York and see where he'd lived all these months and years in seclusion, but of course, very tragically, he wasn't there. I never knew the story would develop, that it would keep on developing like this, because now I'm writing his biography, and learning even more—all the discoveries I'd made in my book *Shout* are not all there is to know about John. And this journey of discovery is still continuing.

Who was he? He was himself—entertainers who know how to be themselves are very, very few, and he himself was this wonderful, naturally funny, sometimes disrespectful and exasperating but always brilliant communicator of color and excitement and humor, and he belonged to the Beatles, this engine of human happiness, which was probably the greatest of modern time. A group who was, and still is, loved. Other rock bands or singers may sell more records or make more money, but none has ever been more *loved* than the Beatles. And if you play a Beatles track to a small child now, as much as any other time in the last forty years, they instantly love it, this quality of love that the Beatles immediately create between them and their audience.

The way he made people laugh, God knows there are few enough people in this world who make you laugh, intentionally, at least, and he was one of them. Dr. Johnson called it "adding to the harmless stock of human merriment," and

John did. But even further, it was the idea that the regression of human civilization and human values which had been going on for the last half century had just taken another leap backwards in a completely illogical brutality. What on earth could be the point? Somebody might, somewhere, have had some kind of perverted motive killing John F. Kennedy, some political motive, but what is the possible motive for killing a man who made music?

John continues to have an extraordinary impact, as a person who is saying with the sort of finality of a child, "I don't care what you say, we ought to have peace." In that sense he's become a secular saint, which of course, he would have thought hilarious—he never wanted or quite expected or pretended to be a saint. He had a sort of invulnerability, in that no one could say anything about him that he wouldn't just as cheerfully say about himself. He did have an honesty that was helpless and involuntary. He liked to achieve peace, he said, we wanted to need it. I mean, how can one respond to that message? It's the simplest, it's the message of all the great religions. And he also had the ability, especially in his later work, to create a primal chant, which is just as effective—or perhaps even more effective—at a mass rally, as at a pop concert.

He stood for anarchy and rebelliousness, rejecting convention. But I'm finding that there was another side, a rather meticulous perfectionist, not all-over-the-place anarchic, which you'll see in the lyrics—he writes absolutely meticulous, perfect lyrics; however simple they may be, they are flawless—the perfectionist side of John Lennon.

Philip Norman is a noted music historian who has written several definitive books on the Beatles including *Shout! The Beatles in Their Generation.*

CYNTHIA O'NEAL

JANUARY 1975 WAS A WINTER OF GREAT SNOWS, A MAGNIFI-
CENT WINTER. WE HAD ONE GLORIOUS CITY-STOPPING BLIZ-
ZARD AFTER ANOTHER. IT WAS ALSO THE TIME WHEN MY
HUSBAND, OUR TWO SONS AND I MOVED INTO A BEAUTIFUL
horizontal apartment in the Dakota from our very nice but vertical
brownstone. Before moving in, there was renovating to do. So for
several weeks I visited the Dakota each day, keeping an eye on the
new kitchen, the new bathrooms, and all the other changes we were
making.

One morning after I had made a brief visit and seen that all was
going well, I left the apartment and rang for the very slow-moving elevator. While I waited, I leaned against the frame of a window that
looked out at the snow, watching the luscious fat flakes as they floated
down. There's an elevator in each corner of the Dakota situated in a
square hallway that also contains a very ornate staircase that leads to
the ground floor and a window looking into the courtyard. From any
of these corner windows, there's a clear view to the apartments across
the way. Given the size of the Dakota windows, it's difficult not to
indulge in a little voyeurism, and at that moment I was particularly
drawn to one, on the other side of the courtyard, which looked into a

big white kitchen. There was a man sitting at a table in the middle of the room, reading the paper and drinking his coffee. The scene, through the soft focus of the snow, was warm and inviting and beautifully still. I stood watching him, mesmerized. Then as I watched, it slowly came to me . . . I was looking at John Lennon. The elevator came, and the elevator went—I couldn't move. There he was.

I'm not sure now why I was so amazed. Certainly I knew that John and Yoko lived in the building. I probably had even heard which floor they lived on. Perhaps it was simply the extreme intimacy of watching him reading his morning paper, drinking his morning coffee, maybe fifty yards away.

Once we were finally living in our new apartment, I settled into a schedule. I got our two boys off to school, then walked down to SoHo where I had a studio. Always, on the way out, I would take a moment to pause by that window, and, almost always, there he would be. If I exited our apartment from the front door, the nearest elevator was the one from which I could see into the Lennon kitchen. However, if I left from the back door, I was nearer to the elevator that John and Yoko used, so there were many times over the next few years when John and I ended up alone together in that small mahogany-paneled box as we rode up or down.

In the course of my long and noisy life I have had the good fortune to know many of the great artists of our time. It's been many years since I was undone by celebrity but I was completely undone by John Lennon's physical presence. I don't know exactly how to describe what it was, something about how he filled the space, his intensity of color, how vividly he stood out against the background as though he were defined by a sharp black outline. Whatever it was, it stopped my breath. I could just barely squeak out, "Hi, how are you?" A few words about the weather and his young son were the limits of my conversations with him. The years passed, and it never got any better.

On the evening of December 8, 1980, my husband was in L.A. working, our sons were in their rooms and I was in my favorite position—lying on my bed, reading. Somewhere at the edge of my consciousness, just outside my book-concentration, I heard some sharp, cracking sounds. A few moments later our older son, Max, came into the room saying, "Mom, did you hear that. Those were gunshots!"

"Don't be silly," I said dismissively and went back to my book. A few moments later, Max was back again. "Mom, I was right . . . those were gunshots . . . John Lennon's been shot . . . I just heard it on the radio!"

No.

No.

I tried to buy a few seconds by getting annoyed with Max and telling him that it was a lousy joke, but of course I knew, the way you know. I remember I thought about racing down the stairs, but I was too late to be of any help. I'd already heard the ambulance, and I knew that he wouldn't be there. I was afraid his blood would be there, and I didn't know how I could bear that.

We turned on the television and watched the horror unfold, terrible detail by terrible detail. As with Kennedy's assassination, I had the desperate, prayerful hope that somehow John Lennon was superhuman, that he could survive such massive damage. With Lennon, I think it was even more quickly that we knew we had lost him. I remember staring at the television screen, watching Yoko leave the hospital.

Despite the icy December cold, thousands of people started arriving outside the building almost immediately. That night was the first of many when I lay in bed, completely awake, eyes wide, listening to the chanting, the mantra, float up from the street below. . . . All we are saying / Is give peace a chance. Over and over and over. Day and night. Some people in the building complained that it kept them awake; I found it very comforting. I liked knowing how many other hearts were broken.

I remember that first night, or rather early morning, lying in the dark and wondering what on Earth it must be like in that other apartment across the courtyard.

For the next three or four days, the atmosphere surrounding the Dakota was incredibly moving and beautiful. It was clear that the people who were there were there out of love. They didn't know how to be anywhere else; they needed to be as close to John as they could get. They continued to weep, to bring armloads of flowers, to light candles, to play Beatles' songs on their boom boxes, to chant. All we are saying. . . . That piece of New York City was transformed into a round-the-clock memorial service—John Lennon was dead.

When we moved into the Dakota, I felt I was moving into the most desirable, most magical building in all of New York City. We lived there for a few more years after that dreadful night, but everything had changed for me; I didn't love being there anymore. Every time I walked through that grand archway, it all came back. Every time.

Cynthia O'Neal is founder and president of Friends in Deed, a nonprofit organization that provides counseling, information and support services for HIV/AIDS, cancer and other life-threatening illnesses.

VICKI PETERSON

JOHN LENNON WAS MY EARLIEST SEXUAL FANTASY. APART FROM PETER PAN, OF COURSE, BUT I'M NOT SURE I SHOULD GET INTO THAT.

IN 1964 I WAS SIX YEARS OLD AND *A HARD DAY'S NIGHT* was playing at the Fox Theatre in Northridge, California. The first time my older sister Pam and I went to see the film, I found the Beatles' thick Liverpudlian accents all but indecipherable. We went back again and again and soon I not only understood the dialogue, but I had it memorized. Sometime during those first Beatles-drenched days I had a dream. An awesome dream. Something about Paul and John having an argument over me (well, *of course . . .*) and John becoming mildly angry and insistent and yet incredibly . . . *sexy.* I woke up with a whole new set of emotions to deal with. Feelings located somewhere in between Fear-of-Dark and Day-at-Disneyland. I did what I sometimes did with a favorite nocturnal dream and expanded it into an elaborate daydream, filling in the story line and just secretly living there for a while. I was trying to imagine what sort of man John Lennon was and why he made me feel so funny inside.

I eventually developed a more typical childhood crush on Paul

McCartney, but John always held a darker, more complex fascination for me. It was as if there was something secret I'd shared with him.

The Beatles' music was so deeply ingrained in my consciousness, it was almost as if it were part of my religious upbringing (I believe that Mr. Lennon once had something to say along these lines). Lennon's songs in particular were absorbed and used as inspiration when I began to write and play my own music. They were personal and honest—not always the easiest songs to swallow. I longed to write something as affective as "Julia" or "You've Got to Hide Your Love Away," or as blithely confessional as "Norwegian Wood." Silly me.

Even Lennon's assassination, as sudden and shocking a heartbreak as it was, became a form of inspiration. On that day in December 1980, my sister Debbi and I were sharing a Hollywood apartment with our lead guitar player, whom we had just fired. Our bass player had recently quit, and the Beatlesque power pop band we'd formed in high school was now down to just my sister and me. We were devastated by the unfathomable loss of our musical hero. We felt adrift and alone—we weren't sure what our next step should be. A week or so after John's death, the phone rang. I answered it and spoke to a young woman who was calling in response to the newspaper ad our ex-guitarist roommate had placed. This woman, a singer and guitarist looking for a band, was a lifelong Beatles fan who had been shaken out of her post-college ennui by John Lennon's murder. The conversation went on for more than an hour, and by the end of it plans had been made to meet and play some songs for each other. That woman was Susanna Hoffs and the band we formed became the Bangles.

Vicki Peterson is lead guitarist and a founding member of the Bangles.

Kate Pierson

John Lennon is practically a mythological figure to me because he loomed so large on my budding consciousness.

I first heard an interview with the Beatles on the radio just before they came to America and I was an instant Beatlemaniac. They almost seemed like the saviors of teenagers—beamed down from another sphere with their cool accents and new hairdos!

My girlfriends and I had a folk protest group called the Sun Donuts, and we each had a favorite Beatle.

John was my immediate favorite because of his sharp, tongue-in-cheek attitude. I still have my yellow-and-black lenticular button that flashes between "I love John" and his picture.

But the thing is, I never grew out of my hero worship, because as John grew up, so did I. After Beatlemania, there was John.

He left the Beatles, found his muse and soul mate, Yoko Ono, and together they formed the Plastic Ono Band that was totally un-Beatles.

He did his own thing, tried to be real and followed his bliss. He made beautiful solo albums and wrote incredible songs. He also had his highs and lows and talked and sang about them.

He became a feminist and let everyone know that Yoko opened up new worlds to him.

John and Yoko were on the forefront of the Peace Movement. He went against the popular grain. He did primal scream therapy, wrote books, drew funny pictures and stayed home to bring up little Sean.

John and Yoko stood for all the things I believed in, and all of us in the B-52's were greatly influenced by John and Yoko.

Then in 1980, while the B-52's were on tour, there was a magazine interview with John where he mentioned the B-52's! I couldn't believe it. He said he'd heard our song "Rock Lobster" (with its obvious Yoko influence) and said to Yoko that it was time for them to make a record again. It was hard to imagine that someone who had influenced me so greatly had actually been affected by something I was a part of.

I had always wanted to meet John, and at that point it seemed maybe someday I would—but soon it would be too late.

But to this day, he still influences me—John is and always will be my working-class hero.

Kate Pierson is vocalist, keyboardist and a founding member of groundbreaking New Wave band the B-52's.

Iggy Pop

I met John in Hong Kong in 1977. He was traveling with Sean, who was about two years old, and was on his way to meet Yoko in Japan. I was with David Bowie and Coco Schwab, his friend and PA, on our way back to Europe from Japan, after a rock tour of my stuff.

David and John were friends, and we learned en route to Hong Kong that he would be there, in our hotel, for the same few days that we were.

A pair of elevator doors opened, and he stood in the hotel hall foyer, wearing a basketball jersey which was WAY too big, and he gave David a very big hug, and a kind of laughing, greeting smile. I was surprised to see an English industry giant exhibit such warmth. Also to see him in a basketball jersey, was super-cool (pardon my fandom).

We went to dinner a couple of times, the four of us, after Sean was in bed for the night. Also to a topless bar once, and once to tea at a snooty country club. He really knew how to sound off when he wanted to, and at each of the latter two destinations rose to his feet to half-yell, half-chortle, "Have You Ever Heard of the Beatles??!!" when service was not forthcoming. I think he enjoyed this. I know I did.

Once we were informed that a restaurant of our choice had a dress code. John would have to wear a shirt. After dinner, which was chicken, he blurted, "Great! You've got to put on a white shirt to eat a dead pigeon!"

He spoke to me directly really only once, to say, "I saw your show in New York. That was pretty good." So he gave me a great gift, casually.

I remember him strolling a half-lit street on the Hong Kong waterfront around midnight, hair in a crewcut, toothpick in mouth, in blue jean pants and jacket, with a lot of space around him in the street, and I think he was enjoying that space. It's a very enduring image in my mind.

Iggy Pop is widely considered the godfather of punk rock. With his band the Stooges, he helped spawn a movement that revolutionized popular music in the early 1970s.

BILLY PRESTON

I WAS VERY YOUNG, BARELY SIXTEEN, WHEN I FIRST MET JOHN. HE AND THE GUYS WERE OPENING FOR LITTLE RICHARD, AND I WAS ON THE TOUR AS RICHARD'S B-3 ORGANIST. THIS WAS THE FAMOUS TOUR WHERE RICHARD, who had turned to be a minister, reverted and played rock-and-roll shows in Hamburg, Germany, in 1962. I'd never played anything but gospel before, having toured before I'd really reached teenage with Mahalia Jackson and then Reverend James Cleveland.

Right from the start, I fell in love with the Beatles; they all were dear to my heart right from the beginning. I was probably their first American "fan" and friend.

John was great—he was funny; he was so smart and clever. I admired him instantly for his wit and manner. You just knew he was special; genius, I suppose, stood out even then, and even to me, a very naïve kid.

As I came to know John and eventually have the pleasure and honor of working with him as a Beatle and then later as a solo artist, I learned he had the great gift to teach, and he was most generous with it. I learned so much from working with and around him, lessons I carry with me even today, subtleties that helped me be successful as both a writer and an artist in my own right.

John actually took the time to teach me how to play the harmonica while we were in Hamburg on that first tour together. The song I learned was "Love Me Do." I reciprocated by making sure that he and George, Paul and Ringo ate. They were only the opening act so they didn't get any meals from the promoter. Richard, being the big American headliner, got steaks and chops and a fabulous spread nightly, so I made sure that the soon-to-be Fab Four were well fed and watered.

One time a few years later when we were in the studio, John sent me out in London in his Rolls to pick up women . . . now wait . . . he wanted a large crowd at Abbey Road so I set out on my mission and filled the Rolls with birds (that's what they were called in England in those years) and took the load back to the studio. Oh my, my.

I don't think any of us who knew and loved John have ever been the same since we lost him. I am sure that both the music world and the world itself have suffered from the absence of his talent and his living presence. His legacy is grand and a true treasure that must pass forward to the next generations.

Billy Preston is a Grammy Award–winning singer-songwriter and pianist who has recorded and toured with such legends as Ray Charles and Sammy Davis, Jr. He worked on *Let It Be, Abbey Road,* and *The White Album,* and is often credited with being the "fifth Beatle." He also appears on several Beatles solo projects including John and Yoko's 1970 release, *Plastic Ono Band.*

JOE RAIOLA

A FEW YEARS AFTER I GRADUATED COLLEGE IN 1977 I
JOINED AN EXPERIMENTAL THEATER GROUP ON MANHAT-
TAN'S UPPER WEST SIDE, JUST DOWN THE STREET FROM
THE DAKOTA, CALLED THE THEATRE WITHIN WORKSHOP. IT
was founded by maverick director Alec Rubin, who was also a primal
therapist. Alec was into working with performing artists on a core
emotional level and helping them create raw autobiographical material for the stage. All of the scenes and monologues we developed in
the workshop grew out of our experience in what Alec called "primal
process."

It's a difficult thing to describe to someone who hasn't actually been
in the therapy. Imagine being shut down and neurotic for twenty-five
years when suddenly everything you've been hiding—your pain, anger,
tears and fears—erupts with volcanic force. It's both liberating and
terrifying.

Of course, it was well known that John had walked a similar path
and we felt a special bond with him. His songwriting had been deeply
impacted by his intensive therapy with *Primal Scream* author Arthur
Janov. The results could be heard on his riveting *Plastic Ono Band*
album, which we loved for its depth of feeling, directness and sim-

plicity: "Mama don't go; daddy come home." "As soon as you're born they make you feel small . . ." "Look at me—who am I supposed to be?" "My mummy's dead; I can't get it through my head." "We're afraid of everyone, afraid of the sun . . ." "Love is real; real is love . . ." "I don't believe in Jesus, Buddha, Beatles—I just believe in me, Yoko and me."

I was fifteen when *Plastic Ono Band* was originally released, and I appreciated the album's searing honesty even then. But listening to it a decade later, just as I was embarking on my own journey in primal therapy and coming of age as a man, it was a total revelation to me. I was roused and inspired by John's vulnerability and his unflinching willingness to express his sadness, anger and pain. He was doing the personal healing work that I aspired to and it had completely transformed him—as a man and an artist. It had nothing to do with his celebrity status or wealth; John grew because he was committed to shining light into the dark places within himself. If he could do it, maybe I could, too. Maybe we all could.

The next year John was gone. I'll never forget that night he died. I was a taxi driver in those days and I was behind the wheel of my cab when I heard the news. I had never lost a dear friend or family member before, so perhaps that's part of the reason John's death hit me so hard. That, and the utter senselessness of it. Instinctively, I flipped on my "off duty" light and headed straight for the Dakota. By the time I arrived a crowd had already gathered. We hugged one another and cried and took whatever comfort we could in singing John's songs.

By 4 AM I was exhausted and in no shape to return home to Queens. So I walked over to Alec's apartment, which was in the neighborhood just two flights above our theater studio. Until then our relationship was that of teacher/pupil, but that morning a friendship was born. We stayed up until dawn talking about John and listening to WNEW-FM where overnight host Vin Scelsa had dispensed with the music and was speaking with callers on the air. Neither of us realized it at the time, but the idea of doing an annual Lennon tribute had taken root in our hearts.

The following summer we were involved with a playwright who was writing a piece about the night John died and how it dramatically changed the course of two couples. We were going to present it as a reading, but a few weeks before it was scheduled to happen, the playwright got cold feet and pulled out of the project. Our impulse to remember John was strong and we felt compelled to do something. But what? We had already sent out publicity and the audience would be expecting a show about John and his impact on our lives. Why not present an evening of theater, dance and music as a tribute to him? That first show was incredibly cathartic for performers and audience members alike. I don't recall who suggested it, but we decided that night to make it an annual event, and after a quarter of a century it's still going strong.

Like anything with a long and vibrant life, the Annual Lennon Tribute has gone through some big changes over the years. It began as an outpouring of sorrow and grief and has evolved into a joyful celebration, not just of John, but of ourselves as performing artists in service to our community. (The show is a benefit for New York's homeless children.) As director, I challenge the performers to take creative risks and develop work that grapples with the same perennial issues that John revisited throughout his career: peace, love, rebellion, spirituality, feminism and personal transformation.

That the show continues to inspire us to create new work in his memory and attract a warm audience every year is a testament to the lasting gift that John left behind. We remember him so fondly because he touched us at the very core of our beings, as only a great artist can.

"While there's life, there's hope," John once said. Well, it turns out there's hope in death too, because the essence of what John embodied can never be snuffed out: it lives on in us.

For me, our Annual Lennon Tribute is an uplifting reminder of that eternal reality.

Joe Raiola is a senior editor at *Mad* magazine. He is also an actor and theatrical director who leads an Annual Lennon Tribute performance each year in New York City.

BONNIE RAITT

FROM THE FIRST TIME I SAW THE BEATLES ON THE *ED SULLIVAN SHOW*, JOHN WAS THE ONE FOR ME. THERE WAS JUST SOMETHING ABOUT HIM — THAT ADORABLE GRIN, SOULFUL VOICE AND JUST PLAIN SEXY PHYSICALITY THAT GOT me bad. Like everyone under the Beatles' spell, I devoured every bit of news, music and film I could get my hands on, suffering my first painfully acute crush. At one point I filled a whole wall of my bedroom in Los Angeles with photos I'd collected of John.

I loved his stance as I did his music, got way into his artwork and poems, the wicked, irreverent wit that skewered hypocrisy and stupidity around him. The Beatles helped shepherd the counterculture revolution, but it was in John's personal arc that I saw my own way modeled. As he blossomed into a solo artist, political activist, devoted lover and father, I got to see how a modern, sensitive man could re-invent himself with new consciousness and rebelliousness intact.

I also think one of his great overlooked legacies will be how he raised up the power of the Feminine—unabashedly championing its power to nurture peace, love and balance as much in himself as in the world. In the way he lived his life, his contributions are monumental. He more than imagined a new way of being—he lived it.

Bonnie Raitt is a Grammy Award–winning singer-songwriter and guitarist. Long an activist for social justice, she cofounded the Rhythm and Blues Foundation in 1988 and has been involved in causes ranging from Native American rights to environmental protection.

PAUL REISER

THE FUNNY THING IS I DON'T REMEMBER ANY *BUILDUP* TO THE BEATLES. WHEN THEY FIRST APPEARED ON THE *ED SULLIVAN SHOW*—OR, AS MY FATHER INSISTED ON CALLING IT, THE "ED *SOLOMAN* SHOW"—I DIDN'T REALLY KNOW IT was coming. My sister mentioned something about "somebody on this Sunday we have to watch." But that was about it.

So we watched. We sat on the floor in front of the big Magnavox TV, Ed introduced the Beatles, and—BOOM—there was John. I didn't pick a "favorite Beatle." I didn't make any choice. He just . . . on some cellular, right-past-the-brain level, he *got* me.

I couldn't tell you what it was, exactly. The voice. The squint. The smile. The way his knees bent out when he was bopping to keep time. The way it seemed like he was really talking to you. . . . When he sang, "She said she loves you"—swear to God—I actually turned to my parents and asked, "She loves who—*me?*"

So okay—I was seven. I was impressionable. But here's the thing; it never went away. From that moment on, I was never *not* aware of John being in my life. He was the Constant. Soothing, surprising, challenging, inspiring, Moving and evolving—but always *there.*

Later, when John and Yoko moved to New York, I suddenly liked my city that much more because they were there, too. You could walk through the park, point to the Dakota and go, "Yup . . . he's right there. In one of those windows. Probably eating eggs and reading the paper right about now." It never failed to make me happy.

Of course, I never *saw* him. Everyone else did. I must have heard a hundred stories from people who bumped into John all over town. Coming out of the movies, waiting for a cab, sitting at Papaya King. . . . Me? Not once. But that was okay; sharing a city was enough. We had that bond. If you had asked me to list everyone who lived in New York, it would be: "Well, let's see . . . there's *me,* John Lennon . . . so that's two right there. . . ."

Now, this may be a tad too revealing, but when I was maybe ten or eleven, I was already concerned about how hard it was going to be later—in my seventies—when we'd inevitably hear on the radio that "former Beatle John Lennon passed away today at the age of eighty-nine" or whatever. Even in *that* scenario, I wasn't looking forward to a world where John Lennon wasn't around.

The night he died, I performed at the comedy club the Improv, on West Forty-fourth Street, a few doors down from the Hit Factory recording studio, where John spent his last night working. (I later calculated that I walked into the club exactly as John walked out of the studio—my last chance to *still* not get to see him.)

When I got offstage, I heard the news. I wanted to believe it was some tragically random street crime, because otherwise it meant somebody shot John Lennon *on purpose.* And well . . . that's . . . that would just be The End Of The World.

So now, it's twenty-five years later. We've actually been without John far longer than we ever had him with us. And no, the world didn't end. But . . .

Selfishly, I think of all the songs we never got to have. And how much we need him. On tough news days, I still think, "Man, if John were around, *he'd* know what to say. *He'd* tell us what to do!"

To which, I'm sure, he'd say, "Hey, man, don't look at me—I'm just a guy." He never wanted to be a hero or anyone's messiah. He was "just a guy." Like you and me.

To which I'd have to say, "Yeah, okay. But . . . not really. You're *John Lennon,* for crying out loud."

Then he'd probably say something else, and finally I'd say, "I get it. I get it. *Of course,* we can't get our answers from you. Or anyone else. *Of course* we've all got to make our own way." But—and this I say to *you,* not to him—Look how much better we can all do that *because* of this "guy." This guy who told us, "Imagine." That "War is over if we want it." That "all we need is Love." And that so, dear friends, we'll "just have to carry on."

So, okay—we will. Fair enough. We'll carry on, and forward we'll march.

But boy, do I wish he was here. This sweet, beautiful friend I never met.

Paul Reiser is an actor and comedian familiar to most for his work as both coproducer and costar of the popular television series *Mad About You.* He has appeared in several films, including *Diner* and *Aliens.*

CARLOS SANTANA

In December 2002 I was invited to play at the Nobel Peace Prize Awards Gala to celebrate the selection of President Jimmy Carter as that year's Nobel Peace Prize honoree. I was both thrilled and honored to participate, most particularly because Mr. Carter is the embodiment of dignity, grace and the hope for a better world.

I knew almost instinctively that we had to include John Lennon's "Imagine" in our song list, for what better song is there for such an august and momentous occasion that celebrates the cause of world peace?

As I reflect upon that wonderful occasion and think about John Lennon, another man of peace, I can't help but feel that "Imagine" was and is a song for the ages, for the quest for peace and harmonious coexistence will always measure the progress of humanity as it defines the quality of our very existence.

In "Imagine" John Lennon said so much that I believe and continue to espouse as fervently and passionately as I am able: the concept of no countries and religions to kill and die for, and the dream of a world without greed or hunger. This is more important today than ever before. Like John Lennon, I envision and pray for a world where the only passport is the heart and where war, hatred and unjustifiable fear and ignorance are banished.

John Lennon was an uncommon man, one who even with all his wealth and fame still chose to recognize and confront the ills of society and to speak out against the madness of war and planetary destruction. Today, some twenty-five years after his senseless death, this country and this world are mired in the same deplorable muck that John railed against in his time. Perhaps the best way to pay tribute to John Lennon is for all of us to recognize that rather than wait for the next John Lennon, that next messenger of world peace, we need to unify and put a stop to the madness and the folly of war and harness our collective will and might in the cause of peace, progress and compassion.

Just imagine what kind of world we could build.

Carlos Santana is a guitarist and songwriter. His unique blend of Latin, jazz and rock music traditions has been a key ingredient in the development of American popular music.

James Manseau Sauceda, Ph.D.

I was teleported into another world through my transistor radio ("transistor" being the prehistoric ancestor to "iPod"). It was February 1964 and I was but a twelve-year-old pod myself, living lost and alonely on the suffering streets of Compton ("Compton"—that's in Cali folks, only a few decades *before* Dr. Dre would create NWA and a gangsta hip-hop beat set to the same heat of those streets). Anyway, what I heard, circa 1964, was pure Technicolor joy.

The profound point the Beatles made was simple: I wasn't *alone anymore*. Why? Because they wanted "To Hold *My* Hand!" (That singular song was so celebratory and empowering.) And who can feel lost and alonely when four people "Love *You*—Yeah! Yeah! Yeah!" Oh, I know it sounds so sentimental now—But it wasn't then; it was Monumental.

Now being a Beatlemaniac in Compton ain't so easy. But my posse (all nonviolent dudes, thank you very much) had an oasis of Hope. Every new Beatles single, and each new LP, opened up new Possibilities for us (and the "us" was worldwide, their magic being electric and ecumenical).

Yet, among the Four Fab's there was, for me, only One who led the brightest brigade ever made: John Lennon. Come on, even in his tailored suit he looked tuff (and you just knew that, inside, he hated wearing them). And right off the bat of the Beatles Bop, I felt John's anger and tension and invention and swagger (something under my own skin shivered in time).

Then came The Books from "the writing Beatle": *In His Own Write* (1964) and *A Spaniard in the Works* (1965). I not only bought them, I chewed and choked on 'em. We all did. Check out the Compton crew tongue-twisting with Liverpool's "Loud Mayor" or us crackin' up and capping with, "The Wonderfoul Larf of Liddypool." Hey, I admit we couldn't "get" a lot of the puns back then, but we sure got the joke! Yes, John's secret langwedge was safe with us. And, boy oh Boi, how Lennon's satire was a Scream (whether in poems, original drawings, short stories or play-as-if-in-a-play scenes). John's pen skewered them all—religion, schools, politicians, etc. et. cicero. As it turns out, years later, I went on to pursue my Master's and Ph.D. degrees studying James Joyce (in Dublin, London and back home at the University of Southern California). In fact, it was while in London that I *nearly* met John Lennon. The date was July 15, 1971, and I had read that J & Y were going to be at Selfridges store downtown for a book signing of Yoko's *Grapefruit*. My nefarious goal was to get John to sign *In His Own Write*, too. But I hopped onto the wrong bus, of curse, so *neither* happened!

After John was stolen from us I needed to give back some small something in thanks for the huge gifts he had given me. I started by creating a course studying John's writing and music, "The Aesthetics of John Lennon" (being one of the first of its kind offered at a major university, USC). Yoko was informed of my modest effort by Elliot Mintz (by then the course was "touring" other universities). But I also wanted to reflect and honor Lennon's literary brilliance in a more substantial way. I could see that a sickening spate of so-called tell all books were fast a-coming (these "tell alls" tell us nothing about John's *real* life, which was, and remains, his *art*). Maybe the best I could do would be to respond from the academic side of the house. Sure, why not offer up a lighthearted look at the overlooked *literature* of this Music Man? Yeah! A bona fide study ("serious," but please *not* somber or stiff). Yeah!! I could then cover *all* of his published poetry and prose, Yeah!!! That's how *The Literary Lennon: A Comedy of Letters* came to be (never heard of it? Well, we small-time scholars seldom attract big-time publishers!). Yoko, however, was approving of the manuscript (which *still* makes me smile). Also, a special moment came when Bill Harry presented an exclusive personal reminiscence of John as "author" for *The Literary Lennon* (Harry being the world's *first* publisher of John Lennon's writings in *Mersey Beat,* circa 1961).

Then, thanks to Mark Lapidos and his "Beatlefests," I was given many a peaceful chance to publicly share the funny findings of Lennon's writing. Beatlefest audiences consisted of avid fans that were also eager to appreciate another side of John's genius. Because of these cool conferences I got to meet and interview many people who were close to John.

Perhaps "Toppermost of the Poppermost" was Pete Shotton, an original member of the Quarry Men. You see, Pete was one of John's best mates and, in fact, helped to inspire Lennon's wicked humor and outlandish drawings. In 1957 John had begun composing *The Daily Howl,* a kind of satiric news magazine. Lennon would often pass new entries of *The Daily Howl* on to Pete while they were in class. John's mischievous mission was to get Pete to totally disrupt the lesson and, even better, outrage the teacher by "howling" out loud in laughter (it often worked). John officially dedicated *The Daily Howl* to his coconspirator Pete. Lennon also *intended* to dedicate his first published book, *In His Own Write* "To Pete—Who Got It First" (but John didn't want to hurt his Aunt Mimi's feelings so he withdrew it at the last minute.) After Pete Shotton had perused *The Literary Lennon,* he told me, and I gleefully quote, "John would have laughed his bollocks off at this!" (I took that as a compliment.)

Because of John's writings I also had the distinct pleasure of meeting Mr. Ray Coleman, whose felicitous pen has given us such deeply felt biographies of John Lennon. Ray was a most gentle and smiling spirit and he was pleased to see that someone had taken the time to acknowledge John's literary accomplishments. Then there was that enchanting raconteur Victor Spinetti, director of *The Lennon Play* at the National Theater Company of Britain and the Beatles' costar in *A Hard Day's Night, Help!* and *Magical Mystery Tour.* Interviewing Victor at length convinced me that Lennon as "playwright" would form an apt sequel to *LL.* (I'm working on it.)

Finally, the finest scholar of all things Beatles, Mark Lewisohn, has offered me (generously and unselfishly) many literary facts, corrections and emendations over the years. We all anxiously await his forthcoming chronicles of the Lads (the first installment is expected, I hear, in 2008).

All of this magnetic wonder came because of one John Winston Lennon. Why even his name changed me, after he married Yoko he became John *Ono* Lennon (that sweet gesture moved me to do the same, adding my Beloved's name to my own). In closing, I must say that the most memorable "memory" I have of John Lennon comes from Our Own Dear Yoko, whose kindness and caring invited the world to hear how Lennon's life stays *Alive* in us—and will *continue* to do so; "it is shining . . . to the end of the beginning. . . ."

James Manseau Sauceda, Ph.D., is director of the Multicultural Center at California State University at Long Beach and author of *The Literary Lennon,* the first serious study of Lennon's writing.

FRED SCHNEIDER

As a kid, I always read and heard that John was the "witty" or "clever" Beatle. He had a dry and incredibly observant sense of humor. His asides and comments were always a highlight of press conferences and interviews. I felt I totally identified with his outlook; I was fairly cynical and sarcastic at a very early age. His books, *A Spaniard in the Works* and *In His Own Write,* are brilliant, and his works turned me on to those of Edward Lear, a true master of verse. John and the other Beatles really created an exciting time for interesting and experimental lyrics in the rock world. All of this was encouraging for me to follow my own writing path from grammar school on. . . . I'll always be a fan of John's work with the Beatles and of all his solo projects, in all their varied and inventive manifestations.

Fred Schneider is vocalist, percussionist, pianist and a founding member of groundbreaking New Wave band the B-52's.

CARLY SIMON

James Taylor and I spent New Year's Eve with John and Yoko and ten other people at the Shun Lee Dynasty restaurant in Manhattan, and I happened to sit next to John. It was the first chance I ever had to sit close to him and study his face and have a good talk. At midnight, everybody put on goofy hats and blew noisemakers, and John had on this little pointed hat that brought all his features, including his nose, into a kind of pointed focus.

I was pregnant with Ben at the time, and John began to give me the compelling, potentially grim story of Yoko's problematic delivery of Sean. It took twenty minutes to tell, and all the while he wore that silly hat—it would have been difficult to take anyone else but John seriously. I was very moved by the loving, ultimately happy story.

On the day Ben was born, when he had barely been brought back to my room to be placed in my arms, a Tiffany porringer was delivered, and it was inscribed: To Benjamin 1-22-77 Love, John, Yoko and Sean. I was amazed at how rapidly and thoughtfully they had reacted to the birth, because it takes two to three weeks to get anything engraved at Tiffany's, and to this day, I cannot imagine how they found out what my son's name was.

I prefer to think that they got the information through some mystical process, because I believe that's something they were both capable of.

Carly Simon is a singer-songwriter, author and activist. Her song "Let the River Run" won Golden Globe, Grammy and Academy awards.

JOHN SINCLAIR

FRIDAY THE THIRTEENTH
for mike liebler

> *any day*
> *can be the lucky one,*
> *or the one with your number*
>
> *written all over it, 123*
> *507 in the poet's case,*
> *walking out*
>
> *the front door*
> *of the penitentiary,*
> *8:30 p.m.*
>
> *14 years ago today,*
> *2 times 7 years the cycle*
> *of struggle, to make it through*
>
> *in one piece, on the yard*
> *or in these streets, "anyone*
> *who can pick up a frying pan*

owns death," burroughs said,
& sometime in new york city
coming back from the recording studio,

walking up to his front door,
john lennon with a gun
stuck in his face,

oh,
oh, sweet giant of song,
with heart of huge dimension

& eyes deep in the sky,
there has to be a day
when each of us must pass

beyond this tedious sphere,
to enter some wondrous place
of which we do not know

whether we're ready or not,
some other place or space
out of time

where no punk with a weapon
will ever press you again
or blow off your face

out of the depths
of his madness, no one
will hold us

against our will
in a cell with bars in front

John Sinclair

& back, 6 feet by 4 feet
by 8 feet high,
no one will take us
out of our natural lives

& send us away from here
by means of some murderous fantasy
in which we are denied

everything we have lived for—
oh please let us die
at the end of our own time

& not before, free
in our world of strife,
let us have life

as long as we can
& please, let there be men
like monk & john lennon

to share of their hearts
& light up our ways
as long as we may live

detroit
friday, december 13 / december 30, 1985

FROM *THELONIOUS: A MONK OF MONK*

John Sinclair is a poet, political activist and scholar. He formerly managed punk rock pioneers the MC5 and is one of the central figures of the counterculture movement of the late 1960s.

On With the Snow! PHOEBE SNOW

I'll never forget my one meeting with John. It was at my first Grammy Awards, and I was the new kid on the block, with my first album, and John and Yoko were there, too. I was a great admirer of his and especially loved his poetry, which was very "Lewis Carroll," absurdist. I had even memorized a poem of his, "I sat belonely down a tree / humbled fat and small. . . ."

I Sat Belonely

I sat belonely down a tree,
humbled fat and small.
A little lady sing to me,
I couldn't see at all.

I'm looking up and at the sky,
to find such wondrous voice.
Puzzly puzzle, wonder why,
I hear but have no choice.

"Speak up, come forth, you ravel me,"
I potty menthal shout.
"I know you hiddy by this tree,"
But still she won't come out.

Such softly singing lulled me sleep,
an hour or two or so.
I wakeny slow and took a peep,
and still no lady show.

Then suddy on a little twig,
I thought I see a sight.
A tiny little tiny pig,
that sing with all its might.

"I thought you were a lady,"
I giggle, well I may.
To my surprise the lady,
got up and flew away.

So there I was backstage being introduced to this artistic hero of mine, in his velvet jacket and beret, and someone said, "John, I'd like you to meet Phoebe Snow," and he gave me this impish look and popped out with, "Ohhhh! On with the Snow!" And I just laughed, I mean here's my favorite poet giving me my own little poem; it was so sweet. I've never forgotten that.

Phoebe Snow is a New York–born singer-songwriter who has recorded and performed with a diverse array of artists, including Mavis Staples and Paul Simon, in a career spanning thirty years.

TOM SNYDER

John and his lawyer appeared one night for the old *Tomorrow* show at the NBC studios in New York. John was in the midst of an effort to avoid deportation from the United States, and his appearance that night was part of that effort. The only memory of the conversation was John explaining to me that part of the reason he entered the music business was to "get a little extra," as he put it. A little extra attention from female fans. My sharper memory is the night he was killed. NBC had the only existing interview with John, and the *Tomorrow* production phones rang through the night, people from every station and network asking permission to air the *Tomorrow* interview in whole or in part. We gave it to all who requested it. That night, I played the whole conversation one last time. After the show, I thought about John's effort to stay in the United States. He did, of course. But through the years I thought of his success to remain in this country a great irony. Had John been deported, he might still be alive today.

Tom Snyder is a former radio and television talk show host best known for his popular *Tomorrow* show, which aired on NBC from 1973 to 1982. John Lennon made his last major television appearance on the show in 1975.

PETE TOWNSHEND

I'M SITTING TO WRITE THIS PIECE IN A SMALL 3 × 5 METRE "CELL" WITH A DOOR WITH A BARRED WINDOW, WHICH LOOKS OUT TO A GARDEN. THE ROOM IS WHITE, BARE BUT FOR A TRESTLE TABLE, CHAIR AND AN UPRIGHT PIANO. THIS is where I come to do the serious stuff, the words and the new chords; I always hope the two may come together as a song.

The sparseness of this room, designed purely to facilitate the blank lightness sometimes required for creativity, is partly inspired by a man called Padre's room in India. He was one of my Spiritual Master Meher Baba's closest male disciples. When on a pilgrimage there in the 1970s I went to visit. His room contained a small desk, chair and a cot. That was all. On the desk were some tobacco tins (he still smoked his own rolled cigarettes). I asked him what he kept in the tins. He said, "In these tins I keep my possessions." Since that visit I have always wanted to live that way: with my possessions in a few small tins. I manage less elegantly with the rock-star equivalent: a few large buildings.

The other inspiration for this "cell" of mine, and which explains its otherwise rebellious piano, was John's white-white-white writing room at his house in Ascot in England. You will be familiar with it from the video of "Imagine," in which Yoko closes the shutters while John sings and plays. That room, grand but simple, was instructive to me: two artists had conferred and agreed to create a white room, with nothing in it but a white piano on white carpet. The very idea of it was inspiring. If only one song had come from that room, and that song happened to be "Imagine" then the whole rather lovely (but unostentatious) house was less an indulgent pop showplace home than a functional workplace: what the Parisian artists I have known call their "Atelier," a word that means quite a bit more than "studio": it suggests that the artist lives wherever he works, and must work wherever he lives.

I sit in my Padre-John-Yoko writing "cell" and think about what to say about John that will matter to you, you who hold this book and look for something that might add a shade to what you feel you already know about John's effect on the world. All I can tell you is that no one has been as important.

I met John just a few times. The first time was when the Who supported the Beatles at a show in Blackpool, England, in 1964. We preceded them and played in front of a curtain behind which John played along with our closing song. The second time was much later. Brian Epstein had summoned me, with Eric Clapton, to be the first two artist-peers to hear "Strawberry Fields" and "Penny Lane," the Beatles' new recordings on an eight-track tape recorder. John was nervous, I remember. He was with Cynthia, his first wife, and she seemed more relaxed than he was. After we had heard the tracks, I was speechless. Eric came to the rescue: "Could we hear it again?" John quoted the Goons when the table was set; he quipped, "Pull up a food." We ate. We chatted. He seemed relieved that "normal" folk like Eric and I knew what he had done and liked it.

Later I saw Yoko, whom I had known about through her connection with my art-school mentor Gustav Metzger, who—with Malcolm Cecil—had inspired me to make destruction a part of my artistic manifesto on stage. She was performing Happenings at various venues around London in 1967. She was outrageous, challenging, inspired and apparently insane. She was one of the first art terrorists, combining deep morality with confrontation and shock. She was also engaging and deeply erotic. It did not surprise me that she and John would find each other. She and I didn't meet face-to-face until 1993 or thereabouts, when Bob Dylan was honoured by CBS at some ceremony in New York. She was with her son, Sean, who is now a friend of mine. I remember being stunned by how young Yoko still looked, and how especially beautiful she had become.

John's artistic and societal role was sharpened by his eventual partnership with Yoko. I find it hard to imagine him without an independent, powerful and effective woman in his life.

Yoko never distracted John from his main function. He had been among the first of us to realize that great pop songwriting from 1967 onward would require more than an ability to entertain and reflect: songs had to change the world and sharpen our perception of it, its wonder and its flaws. Old news for Bob Dylan perhaps, schooled at the feet of Pete Seeger, but for John, and his peers such as I, this was something we hadn't really been prepared or trained for. Music was "postwar," for dancing and as an aid to forgetting. We had both been to art school of course, and I'm certain that helped. One of John's art teachers was Donald Pass, the visionary painter of angels and the "harvest of souls," something Donald claims to have witnessed. Such inspiration and ambition (to recreate a divine revelation) must have inspired the young John almost as much as the Elvis-influenced super-cool Rive-Gauche dress sense of some of his Hamburg-bound buddies.

Hearing "Strawberry Fields" for the first time, and later "Day in the Life" from *Sergeant Pepper,* and "I Am the Walrus" from *Magical Mystery Tour,* I knew that John was also a genius touched by some revelation. He had found a way to communicate to me in divine riddles, abstractions and vignettes of musical impressionism. It was when he began to work with Yoko that his writing became more specific, leaning less toward the poetic hallucinogenics of *Alice in Wonderland* and more to the poetic social conscience of Woody Guthrie. In John's case the reconciliation of those two worlds generated some of the most incredible pop songs ever written.

For me, one song stands above all others from this period: "Happy Xmas (War Is Over)." The music is unashamedly "Christmassy," but also luscious, new, heartening and joyful. The words are challenging and poignant at once: the future can be different, it is in our power to change things, but we must want that change.

That is what I am left with. John and Yoko changed everything, somehow they made an actual difference to the way we live our lives. Without their actions we might have come to believe that we really were the impotent, disenfranchised, powerless and lost peoples embodied in the tragic young life of someone like Kurt Cobain. They taught us that what we say in our primitive pop poetry is of doubtful value if it does not run in precise accord with what we actually do in our daily lives. So Geldof, Bono, Vedder, Springsteen, Baez and all their like, know that every now and then they must do something and be seen to be doing something. This is not to say that you, holding this book, don't do "good" stuff as well—of course you do. But I think if you are holding this book you will probably be one of those who would prefer someone like me, who has a chequered history, sweeping pen and a big mouth sometimes, to actually try to do something about what ails me and what taints the world as I see it. Sometimes my actions get me into trouble. I have to change myself before I can help to change things for anyone else.

Yoko facilitated John's true genius, which was that he was more than just a great and visionary artist in his field, he was—in the world of pop, and ultimately in the international entertainment heart-center that is New York City—also a true *neighbourhood* man. I pay few that particular compliment.

Pete Townshend is founder, songwriter and lead guitarist of rock legends the Who.

KLAUS VOORMANN

"OH KLAUS, I'M SO HAPPY! YOU REALIZE THIS IS THE FIRST TIME SINCE HAMBURG THAT I'M FREE. NO RECORDING CONTRACT, NO MANAGEMENT, JUST FREE AS A BIRD!"

THIS WAS JOHN, SITTING BACK VERY LOOSE ON THE BIG, lush sofa in the Dakota kitchen, wearing a kimono and warm socks. Yoko was sitting at the kitchen table preparing some sushi. Sean was on a big sheepskin carpet on the kitchen floor. My son Otto was right next to him, sitting of course 'cause they both couldn't walk yet. Examining Sean suspiciously. Otto wasn't quite sure if all this and this boy opposite him was okay. Same with Sean. It was very quiet. The two looked at each other, and—as if on command—they started screaming. Yoko and my Cynthia jumped up picked up their loved ones and went off in different directions. Yoko went with Sean into his room and I went over to Otto. Cynthia put him into my arms and the two of us went for a long, slow walk through this wonderful, large apartment. It's an old building, this Dakota house. And these old buildings have these long, tall, dark corridors. This walk calmed my little Otto down a little, but he didn't feel all that happy yet. John came up from behind me and asked very quiet: "Is he okay?"

Boulevard of Broken Strings: a drunk John in Hamburg on a rainy early morning after a long night of playing, trying to wind down, which meant, with John's temperament, overdoing it. One of those bouncers will lure him into one of those joints until he blacks out.

John messing around on a new toy during the recording session for "Baby You're a Rich Man" at Olympic Sound Barns, London.

"Not quite yet," I answered.

"I guess this is all a little much for the little bugger. You've just come from Los Angeles, and Otto must be tired. Couldn't you have picked a name that's a little more Germanic?"

"Cynthia loves that name, and it's an old family name."

"Well, you're excused then," John answered. "Why don't we go in here?" John opened the door to a big room and there was his big, white "Imagine" grand piano. I walked over to the piano, sat down with Otto on my lap and fiddled around a little on the piano keys. And now my little Otto was happy again. "There's a good boy!" John said, and picked up one of those Polaroid cameras that was lying on the mantelpiece. "Let's have a picture of that one." When we were working on the Harry Nilsson LP *Pussy Cats,* we all got one of those Polaroid

In the drawing: MINNY · ME · JIM KELTNER · PHIL SPECTOR · JOHN Listening back to JEALOUS GUY IMAGINE NY · BRIDGES · Klaus Voormann 05

Jealous Guy: John, Jim, Phil and Klaus listening back to the song at Record Plant Studio, New York City.

cameras as a present. So everything in sight was taken a picture of. By the way, the *Imagine* cover was taken with a Polaroid camera. Yoko took a portrait of John and right after that a double exposure, a picture of the sky. I think that's a beautiful idea. I love that cover!

I hadn't seen John for a while. It really was great to see him so relaxed and happy. It looked like the two of us suddenly had more in common then we ever had before, and that's not even including music! So, here I am sitting with my son on my lap playing John Lennon's famous white grand. But it's true—once you have a child and you really care for it, then it seems as if your life starts new all over again. You smell, see, touch, experience differently. You live with and for your child and your family. The great thing about John was he took the time. He didn't rush into the next adventure, do another record or mold plans for the continuation of his career. What did a man like him need a career for? He couldn't give a shit about all this showbiz. Even though sometimes it was hard—like right now as the phone rings.

"Yes? What is it? Who?" Now, John turned to me whispering, "It's Leonard Bernstein. Yeah. Okay. Let me talk to him. Hello, Leonard, yes, I'm fine. Are you fine, too? So we're both fine, that's good. Yes, yes, yes. No, no, no, no, you heard me right. I don't care if it's for the United Nations. Even if it was the Pope, the answer is no! The Beatles are not getting together even if the whole world wants us to! Yes, yes. No, you're not getting the whole band out there, that's for sure. No."

John was relatively patient listening to what Leonard had to say, but after a while he just had to butt in there: "Now wait, wait, wait! Wait a second here. I have no obligation toward anybody. I'm a free individual. I do what I want to do and not what anybody thinks I have to do or I should do. If I change the nappies of my baby, I do it because I want to do it, not because I have to. But I guess that's a little too far-fetched for you to understand. No offense meant. No, I don't have to sleep on it. Thank you. It's a clever idea, though, to pick you of all people to call me up on this issue and try and talk me into it. Good try, but sorry, the answer is no." (Of course I can't remember the whole conversation between the two, but that's roughly what John said.) "You see, Klaus, I get these phone calls all day. Luckily enough, I've got other people taking care of things, but Leonard lives downstairs."

"You mean he has an apartment here in the Dakota building?"

"Yes, he's a good guy and he'll eventually understand. I can't go out there and play with those boys. In particular this one boy. Too much shit went down to make that gig a happy one. And to put a concert together, all the rehearsals, all the aggravation, and the people expect a lot, and if we're not perfect, they will kill us!"

I said, "The difficult thing is the millions of fans out there. Most of them think they own you."

"Yes!" John butted in, "now they really think they created us. You see this here," (and here John was tapping on his chest), "this here is me, John! Not a Beatle, John. That's over, if they like it or not! Now, I'm getting all worked up again. Let's go back in the kitchen. What time is it? Oh yes, I have to check out the bread I put in the oven, and I should put the rice on. Otherwise we won't have anything for dinner. I'll show you how to cook rice the proper way."

During all this conversation, Otto had been sitting under the piano gazing into a crystal glass ball. I picked my lovely boy up and followed John. "Let's have a look at what his friend is doing." John quietly opened the door to Sean's room. We went up to Sean's bed. He was fast asleep. "Isn't he beautiful," John whispered. And so he was. Parents think their child is the most beautiful child in the whole wide world anyway. John tucked him in a little more, and the two happy proud fathers toddled into the kitchen. John took me by the arm and pulled me to the stove. This was John and Yoko's macrobiotic phase, and they took it very seriously. "You are what you eat. An old Indian saying, did you know that?" John looked at me over the edge of his glasses as if he were testing me.

"No," I answered, "but it somehow sounds good." I must say, I myself had very seriously watched over what I was gulping down my throat for some years now. Really since 1970, when I was living at Friar Park with George and Patti. Patti's wonderful cooking turned me into a vegetarian in no time.

"Now, watch me very closely." Out of one of the cupboards, he pulled out a pot, in which he poured in a few hands full of brown rice. "And now comes the important part!" John's face was serious when he filled me in to the art of rice cooking. "Now you have to put your hand on the rice. Like this, you see?" He moved over a little to the side so I could have a better look into the pot. John was putting his right hand into the pot on top of the rice. "Now you pour the water over your hand, but please wash before you do that!"

"You mean the rice or the hand?"

"Klaus, I ask you! Of course the hand. So don't touch the rice with dirty hands." He took a can of water and poured it into the pot. "You only pour as much water into the pot until the back of your hand is covered with water. Now watch me closely—like this." He slowly let the water run over his hand.

"By watching your face, I would assume this is cold not boiling water."

"Very well observed, my boy. Don't try to be funny now. I don't go for German jokes. Now you add a little salt, like this, and then you let the whole thing simmer and when the water has evaporated, then the rice is ready to be eaten."

"And how long will that be?"

John at the Dakota showing me how to cook rice the proper way.

"Roughly about forty-five minutes. Brown rice needs much longer than that bleached white stuff." John's eyes sparkled with enragement.

"Did you know that you get depressions from white rice? Did you? I'll give you this book called *Sugar Blues*. I promise you when you read this book, you won't touch a piece of sugar again. The kids in school should be forced to read this book. They try to manipulate us all and make us sick. This time the sweet way."

I changed the subject to talk a little about music for a change. "Oh Klaus, it's not like it was anymore. There's no balls in all that stuff any more. Listen to our Bob Dylan. All he does is love songs: 'lay across my big brass bed' and such! Where is the message? Where is the revolution? We all have a vocation, a duty!" John very excitedly wiggled around with his cooking spoon.

"Don't you have to stir this?" I asked.

Breakfast with John.

John stopped his excited talk for a moment, gave the pot a quick look and continued talking.

"No, no, I told you. If you do it the way I told you with pouring the water over your hand, nothing can happen—and don't dare stir the rice! You're gonna make it all 'mushi, matchi.' "

John put the cooking spoons to the side, picked up two clean kitchen towels, opened the oven and took out his loaf of bread. He put it on a wooden board. It really smelled delicious.

"Just listen to his voice on the new record. He sounds all soft and sweet. There is no bite to it. I tell you, it's not like it was before." He lifted the lid and with a pleased look on his face proclaimed: "I think we can eat now, the rice is finished."

The Beatles often played until four, five or six in the morning and went to sleep whenever they could. If you don't get to bed until seven, you usually want to sleep until three. It was like a whole day's work, or in their case a whole night's work. The daytime was for sleeping because, by eight or nine o'clock, they had to be back in the club again. At the end of these shifts, the boys would be very tired and often enough they fell straight into bed. However, there were other times when the adrenaline level wouldn't allow this to happen. If we were still up, we'd go for something to eat. That way we could hang out at Harald's, Chug-Ou's or any of the many other coffee shops. In which case, fitting in with the time of day meant going for breakfast. That was usually very amusing.

Everybody would be wound-up and getting very silly before the crash. Once, that crash happened to John in the middle of his breakfast. The others had already conked out, leaving John and I together—the "last of the mohicans"—sitting it out at Chug-Ou's, where a few other customers sipped their coffee before the morning's work. John was right in the middle of telling a funny story, excitedly fidgeting around with a burning cigarette, when suddenly he stopped, grunted something and let his head fall to his food-filled plate. I laughed, thinking it was another one of those "typical John" jokes, but his head stayed in that position. His eyes remained closed and his breathing was getting heavy. Then he started snoring. I looked around, not knowing what to do, being a little worn-out myself. I was even worried he might have hurt himself, what with his knife laying so near to his eye. When I saw the ash falling from the burning cigarette, which was still perched in his hand, I decided to leave him the way he was. "At least he'll wake up," I thought, "when the cigarette burns down to his fingers." I began thinking of the lovely fried egg on the plate. . . . My God, what one thinks when an unexpected situation comes up! After a few minutes passed, he woke up, swearing like mad because of his burned fingers, and started to eat his spiegelei as if nothing had happened.

"That's ice cold, that junk!"

Klaus Voormann is a musician, artist and graphic designer whose early friendship with the Beatles led to a lifelong creative partnership. He designed the cover art for both *Revolver* and the *Beatles Anthology* project, and recently released the visual retrospective *Hamburg Days* with his friend photographer Astrid Kirchherr.

Loudon Wainwright III

Not John

The limousine was waiting outside the studio
In stepped poor John
Lennon and his wife Yoko
Oh no, not John

On up 44th Street left at 8th Avenue
Up to the Dakota
a man waits there for you
Oh no, not John

The man's name it is Chapman comes from Honolulu
He really loved your music John
Got a Japanese wife too
Oh no, poor Sean

Five bullets in your body that's what the experts say
They say you signed an autograph
For him on that very day
Oh no, not John

There was a vigil at the Roosevelt at the Dakota too
Silence in Central Park
They had a riot in Liverpool
Oh no, not John

Chapman's in the jailhouse. What's he doin' there?
He went and he shot John Lennon
All you heroes best beware
Oh no, not John

Suzzy and I walked out of the movie theatre in Times Square and got lucky, managing to hail a cab right away. The movie we'd seen was *Ordinary People,* and I hadn't much liked it. On a day or a night like that you remember those kinds of details. Days and nights that "live in infamy": December 7, 1941; November 22, 1963; September 11, 2001; and that very night—December 8, 1980.

In the back of the cab I started trashing Redford's movie while Suzzy defended it. Then we were interrupted by the driver with the news that several avenues uptown were closed to traffic. Apparently somebody had been shot. Somebody famous, some guy called John Leonard. "John Leonard," I said to Suzzy, "isn't he that writer for the *New York Times?*" "An English guy," the driver said, correcting me. "Somebody in a band." Then from the backseat we asked our terrible question, "Do you mean John Lennon from the Beatles?" "Yeah, that's the guy," was the answer. We asked him to turn on the radio, and then it was true. When we got home we listened for most of the night. Television would have been too hard—to see a picture of the living John would have been too painful. WNEW was playing the music. Vin Scelsa, Dave Herman, Scott Muni, Pete Fornatale and the others played the music and talked themselves and the tristate area through the ordeal for the next seventy-two hours.

Way before that, when I was a kid, I used to sing an old folk song about the assassination of President McKinley. It started off:

Hey Mr. McKinley why didn't you run?
See that man a comin'

With a Johnson 41
From Buffalo to Washington

I had that song and its descriptive technique in mind when I wrote "Not John." I was trying to tell a story by recounting dreadful details and cold historical facts, attempting to make sense of something that shouldn't have happened by reporting it. And of course such stories need to be reported. Otherwise who will remember the make and caliber of McKinley's assassin's gun or the fact that Mark Chapman was from Honolulu and also had a Japanese wife?

Loudon Wainwright III is a folk musician known for his confessional style and wry sense of humor. In the late 1960s, he was one of many performers to be branded "new Dylan."

ROLLING STONE

NOVEMBER 9, 1967
VOL. I, NO. 1

MFP

OUR PRICE:
TWENTY-FIVE CENTS

Recognize Private Gripeweed? He's actually John Lennon in Richard Lester's new film, How I Won the War. *An illustrated special preview of the movie begins on page 16.*

Tom Rounds Quits KFRC

Tom Rounds, KFRC Program Director, has resigned. No immediate date has been set for his departure from the station. Rounds quit to assume the direction of Charlatan Productions, an L.A. based film company experimenting in the contemporary pop film.

Rounds spent seven years as Program Director of KPOI in Hawaii before coming to San Francisco in 1966. He successfully effected the tight format which made KFRC the number one station in San Francisco.

Les Turpin, former program director of KGB in San Diego will replace Tom Rounds at KFRC. Turpin has spent the last year as a consultant in the Drake-Chenault programming service.

The new appointment could mean a tightening up of programming policies. Rounds liberalization of KFRC's play-list may well become more restricted.

THE HIGH COST OF MUSIC AND LOVE: WHERE'S THE MONEY FROM MONTEREY?

BY MICHAEL LYDON

A weekend of "music, love, and flowers" can be done for a song (plus cost) or can be done at a cost (plus songs). The Monterey International Pop Festival, a non-profit, charity event, was, despite its own protestations, of the second sort: a damn extravagant three days.

The Festival's net profit at the end of August, the last date of accounting, was $211,451. The costs of the weekend were $290,233. Had it not been for the profit from the sale of television rights to ABC-TV of $288,843, the whole operation would have ended up a neat $77,392 in the red.

The Festival planned to have all the artists, while in Monterey, submit ideas for use of the proceeds.

In the confusion the plan miscarried and the decision on where the profits should go has still not been finally made.

So far only $50,000 has definitely been been allocated to

anyone: to a unit of the New York City Youth Board which will set up classes for many ghetto children to learn music on guitars donated by Fender. Paul Simon, a Festival governor, will personally over see the program.

Plans to give more money to the Negro College Fund for college scholarships is now being discussed; another idea is a sum between ten and twenty thousand for the Monterey Symphony.

However worthy these plans, they are considerably less daring and innovative than the projects mentioned in the spring: the Diggers, pop conferences, and any project which would "tend to further national interest in and knowledge and enjoyment of popular music." The present plans suggest that the Board of Governors, unable or unwilling to make their grandiose schemes reality, fell back on traditional charity.

The Board of Governors did decide that the money would be given out in a small number of

large sums. This has meant, for instance, that the John Edwards Memorial Foundation, a folk music archive at the University of California at Los Angeles, had its small request overlooked.

In ironic fact, what happened at the Festival and its financial affairs looks in many ways like the traditional Charity Ball in hippie drag.

The overhead was high and the net was low. "For every dollar spent, there was a reason," says Derek Taylor, the Festival's PR man and one of its original officers.

Yet many of the Festival's expenses, however reasonable to Taylor, seem out of keeping with its announced spirit. The Festival management, with amateurish good will, lavished generosity on their friends.

• Producer Lou Adler was able to find a spot in the show for his own property, Johnny Rivers; Paul Simon for his friend, English folk singer Beverly; John Phillips for the Group Without A Name and Scott MacKenzie. None of them had the musical

Airplane high, but no new LP release

Jefferson Airplane has been taking more than a month to record their new album for RCA Victor. In a recording period of five weeks only five sides have been completed. No definite release date has been set.

Their usual recording schedule in Los Angeles begins at 11:00 p.m. in the evening and extends through six or seven in the morning. When they're not in the studios, they stay at a fabulous pink mansion which rents for $5,000 a month. The Beatles stayed at the house on their last American tour.

The house has two swimming pools and a variety of recreational facilities. It's a small small little paradise in the hills above Hollywood. Maybe suntans and guitars don't make it together.

status for an international pop music festival.

It is ironic that the Rivers and the rest appeared "free," but the money it cost the Festival to get them to Monterey and back, feed them, put them up (Beverly
—Continued on Page 7

Jann Wenner

John was a volcanic genius. He was an explosive personality, full of energy and rages and passions and enthusiasms. Not an easily parse-able man.

We put him on the first cover by sheer accident, really. We were coming down to the deadline and we were looking at what we had in pictures. We had some publicity stills of Private Gripweed in the Richard Lester movie *How I Won the War* and they looked cool so we put it on the cover. It wasn't a premeditated thing—necessity was the mother of invention. It was just the best picture we had, and the most interesting, but how fortuitous! How fricking fortuitous!

I guess our relationship really started over *Two Virgins*. I was twenty-one. They'd banned this record. Ralph Gleason had said, "Hey, look, why don't we get ahold of this picture and print it?" I knew Derek Taylor, who was very close with John because they were both the literary types and the wits, so I wrote to him and said "Can we do it?" and sure enough they did it. They sent us over the *Two Virgins* cover, both sides, and we printed it. It was our first anniversary issue. We'd been around a year, it was issue number twenty-two and it sold out. We had to go back and print some more.

We were a small magazine then, but it was obviously our biggest seller to that date and we got our first little bit of publicity. In the *San Francisco Chronicle*, I remember it very well because the headline on the story was "Naked Beatle Imperils S.F." And I thought, God that is witty, witty, witty. And then I wrote a little editorial, a letter to our readers, in the next issue about our experience of having printed this thing and said "the lesson from all this is print a famous foreskin and the world will beat a path to your door."

The fact that John and Yoko did that naked cover was just staggering because nobody was doing it at that time. Now it's kind of de rigueur, but for them to do it was remarkable on three levels: First, at that time frontal nudity was just unheard of. Second, that a star of his dimension, possibly the biggest star in the world, was doing it. Third, these are not buff bodies. It's like telling people, have the courage to be yourself. Be open, be honest, whatever you look like, it's cool. You don't have to be a Playboy bunny or a buffed-out Marlboro Man. Just be yourself, you're cool, be open about it.

From then on, we were always carrying news about John and Yoko's activities. The Beatles hadn't officially broken up yet but they were really operating separately and John was kind of chomping at the bit. And he kept saying, "Someday I'll tell you my story, someday I'll tell you my story."

They went on their peace crusades and they got married in 1969 in Gibraltar. They went to Amsterdam and Montreal doing the bed-ins. Meanwhile, we were also covering Yoko's avant-garde work. I had a dear friend of mine from college living in London named Jonathan Cott, who really understood all this, understood Stockhausen, classical music and contemporary music. He was writing for *Rolling Stone* and he formed a relationship with Yoko, and with John through Yoko. So we began carrying news of her activities, as well as what John was doing.

When they started doing the peace events, we began to give them much more extensive coverage. It was one of the news stories we followed all the time. Kind of "Dateline Toronto"—here's what they're doing, our reporter or a freelancer would cover it, or John and Yoko would call in, or I would call them, and they'd give us a little interview on the phone, or we'd print the reports and their interviews about their latest activities. Besides the occasional local press or underground paper, we were the main outlet getting to their audience, so we became allies.

ROLLING STONE

ACME No. 22 NOVEMBER 23, 1968 THIRTY-FIVE CENTS
UK: 3/6

The Rolling Stone Interview
With John Lennon

Inside: The Complete
John & Yoko Record Cover

Big Brother and Cream
In Their Last Days

Forty Pages Full
Of Dope,
Sex
&
Cheap
Thrills

And they were both naked,
the man and his wife, and were
not ashamed.

JOHN LENNON

I was in San Francisco and they were in London. I had a little Teletype installed in my office in the printer's loft where our offices were located. It was one of those international private teleprinters (they're in junk heaps everywhere these days). They had one in Ascot, so we'd communicate with whoever their assistant was at the time. We'd send messages back and forth, there's a file full of them, about things having to do with the magazine, statements they were making, or news. I was building a relationship with them and they were trying to get their information out. This brought legitimacy and heightened the profile of the then-emerging *Rolling Stone* and through the course of this came the relationship which eventually led to the famous interview and the book *Lennon Remembers* (Rolling Stone Press, 1971).

The most interesting times I spent with John were when he came to San Francisco in the spring of 1970. He and Yoko called out of the blue and said they were in town. They came down to the office, creating quite a stir with the staff while I was giving them a tour of the *Rolling Stone* offices. They were checked in at the Hilton Hotel in San Francisco, so I immediately stopped work and spent the weekend with them. We moved them to a much nicer, quieter, more private hotel, and we spent the weekend with them seeing movies, walking the streets of San Francisco and going out to dinner. It was interesting to see John, to really see him in action. He was just starting primal scream so his feelings were all at the edge, all on the surface, and he was into this idea of honesty with everything and he refused to hide his feelings. If someone came up to him to bother him for an autograph, he would get offended and pissed off instead of politely dealing with it. I was really surprised with the vituperativeness with which he'd deal with some of these autograph seekers. It would have been easier to sign them, but he said, "Can't you see I'm eating!" and "Yes, you are bothering me!" But, we ought to remember, he was twenty-nine years old then. Pretty damn young. It's often much closer to adolescence than it is to adulthood.

So, we had this wonderful time visiting in San Francisco, where Yoko had spent a little bit of her childhood. We were just two couples touring and having a lot of fun in the city. The most remarkable thing was they had never seen *Let It Be*. So we all went to see it. It had been released about three months earlier. We went one afternoon during the week—nobody goes to the movies in the afternoon—so we were in this completely empty theater, just the four of us all huddled together watching this film about the breakup of the Beatles. It was very painful because it shows their relationships deteriorating and how the Beatles ended. It was quite sobering to be there watching it with the leader of the Beatles. Afterward, we all walked out of the theater and just spontaneously hugged and cried.

When we did the actual interview it wasn't done at home in a relaxed situation. It was all done in Allen Klein's office in New York, in his very official conference room. Klein had his tape recorder going and I taped as well, while Yoko sat in on it.

It was a very big deal in everybody's mind because John hadn't given an interview like that before, *ever*. He'd given little bits of interviews on the fly: a little bit here and there but he was just coming out of that manufactured Beatles-image era and he was just dying to do this, to burst out and finally say something about himself and his experiences, which had really been covered up or kept quiet or kept very sanitized.

You'd see little peeks of him for years, his little statements about being more popular than Jesus, or a little bit of controversy about the Queen, or his wit, but this whole acerbic and very serious side of him had been kept pretty quiet, not to mention his deep unhappiness still being in the Beatles. What was he called— "the Smart Beatle"? All this was bubbling under the surface, you could see it throughout his career, all the things he was thinking and exploring, even from his report cards in school. All of this was just dying to get out, and nobody had ever had the opportunity to do it, so there was quite a lot to ask him about. What was it like to be in the Beatles? Who wrote what songs? What were all the songs about?

We were very young—I was twenty-four and John was thirty—so there are a lot of rough edges, a lot of naïveté, we were all full of ourselves. In retrospect, the interview suffers from my still-developing skills as an interviewer—lack of both methodology and a methodical approach—but perhaps that is why the conversation was so passionate, unnerving and honest. It's him. It's the first really raw, unpolished, frank exposure of him and his real self to the world.

His relationship with the media was actually pretty good. He was receptive, he liked the attention, he liked the publicity, and he had something he wanted to say very much: the peace crusade. He liked talking and he was a great interview—

colorful and open. He also liked to sell records and be on top of the charts—he was very frank about that, too. He enjoyed giving the interviews, he enjoyed the reporters. He didn't suffer fools lightly, and a lot of reporters are fools, but he handled them with charm and, of course, the Beatles were still this romantic, sugar-coated myth. The publication of the interview in *Rolling Stone* was the first time any of the Beatles, let alone their founder and leader, stepped outside that protected world and told the truth. Because he had a sympathetic vehicle in me and *Rolling Stone,* John poured out the truth with the spontaneity, urgency and lack of caution of doing so for the first time. He gave a running commentary on fresh and vital matters, full of the passion and wit that filled nearly everything he did. It was a rare self-portrait of the artist, the likes of which I have not seen since.

People idolized John. He was being persecuted by the Nixon administration and he had been persecuted by the religious crusaders early on, so naturally sympathy went to him. He always got the benefit of the doubt. As cuckoo as a lot of the media thought the bag-ins and bed-ins were, I think people thought, "Well, you know John, he's an eccentric, he's not *harming* anybody," and they *liked* him. He wasn't one of these people to fight them, pretending he didn't want to be in the papers or having a public relations operation going on, all this crap you see today.

I'm sure that he did have a few secrets, but he was remarkably open. I think he felt "What was the point of lying?" He was committed to this idea of openness and honesty, however painful it was going to be. He was an emotional and volatile person who was also very angry at certain things. He just hated hypocrisy and would go out of his way to point it out.

I think people don't recall or remember how painful all this was for him. And how deeply he felt all these ideas and how important the message of peace and love, and those values, were to him. During the Beatles and in the ensuing years of fame, look at what he was writing about. "All You Need Is Love"—these are the concepts and themes, at a level that is too much forgotten. He was a Bertrand Russell, Albert Einstein, committed genius type who was dedicated to this idea of peace and brotherhood.

He died before this all got too fashionable. He set the stage for people like Geldof and Bono.

I wasn't around for the period when he was raising Sean, but I would imagine that the world doesn't remember him as a totally devoted father. Today, it's very fashionable for fathers to participate actively in their child's life and to raise the kids and take on a role, whether they are single fathers or parents. The other traditional model has been shattered. A father is now required to be a nurturing parent, whereas before it wasn't that way, at least not in the intense way that John was.

A tremendous amount of stuff came out of his pain, as a way of solving it. The pain having to do with his childhood, obviously, being in Liverpool with memories of the war, being abandoned by his parents. He was this remarkable individual personality stuck in what must have been a really closed, post–World War II, narrow-minded society in Liverpool that he was constantly fighting against. That was not the land of opportunity, not a home for creative geniuses, which John was from day one of his childhood. I'm sure he suffered the painful memory of that all his life, constantly engaged in a battle with people in authority or people who were culturally oppressive, to him directly or indirectly. People who withheld love, and people who said, "You can't do this" and "You can't do that." Classic rebel.

John is obviously one of the great composers, songwriters, singers and social critics of all time. The Beatles were at the level of sheer genius in singing, melody and songwriting in the era of modern communications, and they were the first with worldwide impact. You could say there were other genius songwriters, whether Gilbert and Sullivan, Rogers and Hammerstein or Cole Porter, but nothing like this had ever happened. They came along at a particular era in social history, and in the history of the world, which was the postwar baby boom. They became, in effect, the spokespeople and representatives of all the yearning of the population that exploded after World War II in Western society and Western-influenced society. They represented the youth culture that is now the dominant, majority population group in the world. They influenced them, they spoke for them, and they set those values in motion. And it goes on today. We know the work, and quite a remarkable body of work, and then that body of work is informed by a social conscience of John's, which he kept pursuing in his solo work both in the studio and outside the studio for years and years and years.

The John Lennon people remember is filtered through an image of a peace-loving, martyred hero, but at his core he was one of the greatest rockers who ever lived. John grew up with Elvis as his idol and if anyone could have succeeded that primal, black-leather-jacketed King, it was John Lennon. That is the legacy that meant more to John than anything else.

—As told in an interview

Jann Wenner is founder, editor and publisher of *Rolling Stone* magazine. He is also chairman and CEO of Wenner Media, which publishes *US* and *Men's Journal* in addition to housing the Wenner Books imprint. He conducted a lengthy interview with John Lennon for *Rolling Stone* in 1970.

The John Lennon FBI Files   JON WIENER

EARLY IN 1981, SHORTLY AFTER JOHN LENNON'S MURDER ON DECEMBER 8, 1980, I FILED A FREEDOM OF INFORMATION REQUEST FOR ANY FILES THE FBI MIGHT HAVE ON LENNON. I DIDN'T REALLY KNOW IF THEY HAD ANY. THE FBI responded in May, releasing some documents and withholding 199 documents in their entirety—out of a total of 281 they said they had reviewed. That meant that more than 70 percent of the documents were withheld in their entirety, mostly under the claim that releasing them would endanger national security.

The documents that were released all dated from 1971–72, when John and Yoko had moved to New York, when the war in Vietnam was at its peak and when Nixon was running for reelection. All of the Lennon FBI file was about Lennon's antiwar activism that year, and his efforts to help defeat Nixon. The file also discusses the Nixon administration's effort in 1972 to deport Lennon, including a letter suggesting that Lennon be "arrested if at all possible on possession of narcotics charge," which would make him "immediately deportable"; and several pages completely blacked-out from the Detroit FBI reporting on John and Yoko's appearance at the "John Sinclair Freedom Rally" in Ann Arbor in December 1971. Most interesting

9-25-97
CLASSIFIED BY SSA5668 SLD/JS
DECLASSIFY ON: 25X 6
CA# 83-1720

CLASSIFIED DECISIONS FINALIZED
BY DEPARTMENT REVIEW COMMITTEE (DRC)
DATE 2/12/86

SECRET

CONFIDENTIAL

2/13/96

CLASSIFIED BY SSA 9803 ROD/JS
REASON: 1.5 (b)(d)
DECLASSIFY ON: X

April 25, 1972

BY LIAISON

CA# CV
83-1720
94-1673
SPACH/MLT

1 - Mr. A. Rosen
1 - Mr. T. E. Bishop
1 - Mr. E. S. Miller
1 - Mr. R. L. Shackelford
1 - Mr. T. J. Smith (Horner)
1 - Mr. R. L. Pence

Honorable H. R. Haldeman
Assistant to the President
The White House
Washington, D. C.

CLASSIFIED DECISIONS FINALIZED
BY DEPARTMENT REVIEW COMMITTEE (DRC)
DATE 12/10/97   SSA5668 SLD/JS 12/10/97
CA# 83-1720

Dear Mr. Haldeman

John Winston Lennon is a British citizen and former
member of the Beatles singing group. ▮▮▮▮▮▮▮▮▮▮▮▮

(C)

Despite his apparent ineligibility for a United States
visa due to a conviction in London in 1968 for possession of
dangerous drugs, Lennon obtained a visa and entered the United
States in 1971. During February, 1972, a confidential source,
who has furnished reliable information in the past, advised that
Lennon had contributed $75,000 to a newly organized New Left
group formed to disrupt the Republican National Convention.
The visas of Lennon and his wife, Yoko Ono, expired on
February 29, 1972, and since that time Immigration and
Naturalization Service (INS) has been attempting to deport
them. During the Lennons' most recent deportation hearing at
INS, New York, New York, on April 18, 1972, their attorney
stated that Lennon felt he was being deported due to his
outspoken remarks concerning United States policy in Southeast
Asia. The attorney requested a delay in order that character
witnesses could testify for Lennon, and he then read into the
court record that Lennon had been appointed to the President's
Council for Drug Abuse (National Commission on Marijuana and
Drug Abuse) and to the faculty of New York University,
New York, New York.

Tolson
Felt
Campbell
Rosen
Mohr
Bishop
Miller, E.S.
Callahan
Casper
Conrad
Dalbey
Cleveland
Ponder
Bates
Walkart
Walters
Soyars
Tele. Room
Holmes
Gandy

RHP:plm
(8)

100-469910

SECRET   CONFIDENTIAL

EC-105

100-469910-7

19 APR 26 1972

SEE NOTE PAGE TWO

DELIVERED BY LIAISON
ON 4/6/72

70 MAY 1 1972

MAIL ROOM ☐   TELETYPE UNIT ☐

Group 1
Excluded from automatic
downgrading and
declassification

CONFIDENTIAL

CLASS. & EXT. BY
REASON-FCIM II.
DATE OF REVIEW

31

Honorable H. R. Haldeman

A second confidential source, who has furnished reliable information in the past, advised that Lennon continues to be a heavy user of narcotics. On April 21, 1972, a third confidential source in a position to furnish reliable information advised that there was no information available indicating that Lennon has been appointed to the National Commission on Marijuana and Drug Abuse. A fourth confidential source in a position to furnish reliable information advised that Lennon has been offered a teaching position at New York University for the Summer of 1972.

This information is also being furnished to the Acting Attorney General. Pertinent information concerning Lennon is being furnished to the Department of State and INS on a regular basis.

Sincerely yours,

NOTE:

Classified "Confidential" since information is contained from █████████████████████████████████████

b1   first confidential source is █████████ second
b2   confidential source is ████████ third confidential source is
b7c   pretext inquiry by WFO with █████████████████████████████
b7D   ████████ National Commission on Marijuana and Drug Abuse,
Washington, D. C.; and fourth confidential source is ████████
████████, New York University, New York, New York.

See memorandum R. L. Shackelford to Mr. E. S. Miller, 4/21/72, captioned "John Winston Lennon, Security Matter – New Left," and prepared by RLP:plm.

was that letter from J. Edgar Hoover to H. R. Haldeman, assistant to the president, dated April 25, 1972, that had been withheld in its entirety under the national security exemption. Since Haldeman was the closest official to Nixon, this document provided crucial evidence that the Lennon investigation was a political one, significant to the highest levels of the Nixon White House.

When these documents began arriving in my mailbox in the spring of 1981, American politics was beginning a shift toward the right of historic proportions. Ronald Reagan had been elected in November 1980, bringing to power the Republican right wing that had failed to elect Goldwater sixteen years earlier. The "Reagan Revolution" rested on an ideological commitment to "law and order," which Lennon had challenged, and a passionate hostility to "the sixties," which Lennon had personified. The fight for the Lennon files would begin as a battle with the new Reagan administration.

When the FBI informed me they were withholding 70 percent of the Lennon files, I concluded that it was time to find a lawyer. Mark Rosenbaum of the ACLU of Southern California and Dan Marmalefsky agreed to take the case.

With their help, I filed a lawsuit under the Freedom of Information Act (FOIA) in 1983 asking the court to order the release of the withheld pages. Fourteen years later, in 1997, after the case went to the Supreme Court, the Clinton Justice Department agreed to settle almost all the outstanding issues of the case, to release all but ten of the documents, and to pay $204,000 to the ACLU for court costs and attorneys' fees. Twenty years later, in October 2004, our judge, Robert S. Takasugi, ordered the FBI to release the last ten pages. The law gave the FBI sixty days to appeal. As of this writing (October 2004), the FBI had not announced whether or not it would appeal.

The Lennon FBI files document an era when rock music seemed to have real political force, when youth culture challenged the status quo in Washington, when the president responded by mobilizing the FBI and the Immigration Service to silence the man from England who sang "Give Peace a Chance." The Nixon administration learned that he and some radical friends were talking about organizing a national concert tour to coincide with the 1972 election campaign, a tour that would combine rock music and radical politics, during which Lennon would urge young people to register to vote, and vote against the war—which meant, of course, against Nixon.

The impetus for the Lennon FBI file came from an unlikely source: Senator Strom Thurmond, who in early 1972 sent a secret memo to Attorney General John Mitchell and the White House reporting on Lennon's plans, and suggesting that deportation "would be a strategic countermeasure." That was exactly the sort of thing John Dean, the counsel to the president, had suggested in his famous 1971 memo: "We can use the available political machinery to screw our political enemies." The word was passed to the Immigration and Naturalization Service (INS), which began deportation proceedings a month later.

The story of the Lennon files is also the story of the twenty-year legal battle to win release of the withheld pages, a story about the ways the Reagan, Bush senior, Clinton and Bush junior administrations resisted the requirements of the Freedom of Information Act. The basic issue here was not simply John Lennon. The basic issue was that government officials everywhere like secrecy. By keeping the public from learning what they have done, they hope to avoid criticism, hinder the opposition and maintain power over citizens and their elected representatives. Classified files and official secrets lie at the heart of the modern governmental bureaucracy, and permit the undemocratic use of power to go unrecognized and unchallenged by citizens.

Democracy, however, is not powerless before this practice. In the fight against government secrecy, America has led the world. The Freedom of Information Act, passed by Congress in 1966, created a notable challenge to the history of government secrecy: a set of rules and procedures, officials and offices dedicated not to the collection and maintenance of secrets, but rather to their release to the public. Journalists, scholars and activists have used the FOIA to expose official misconduct and lying, including the FBI's illegal efforts to harass, intimidate, disrupt and otherwise interfere with lawful political actions. The John Lennon FBI files provide an example.

Throughout the litigation over the files, beginning in 1983, the FBI maintained that their surveillance of Lennon was not an abuse of power, but rather a legitimate law enforcement activity. It's true that in 1972 Lennon associated with antiwar activists who had been convicted of conspiring to disrupt the Democratic National Convention four years earlier. It's true that he spoke out against the war at rallies and demonstrations. But the files contain no evidence that Lennon committed any criminal acts: no bombings, no terrorism, no con-

NR 044 NY CODE

821PM NITEL 5-16-72 KPR

TO ACTING DIRECTOR (100-469910)

FROM NEW YORK (100-175319) (P)

JOHN WINSTON LENNON. SECURITY MATTER DASH REVOLUTIONARY

ACTIVITIES.

 Reference Teletype
RENYTEL MAY THREE LAST.

 ON MAY SIXTEEN INSTANT, VINCENT SCHIANO, CHIEF TRIAL

ATTORNEY, INS, NYC, ADVISED SUBJECT AND WIFE, YOKO ONO,

ARE SCHEDULED FOR HEARING ON DEPORTATION PROCEEDINGS MAY

SEVENTEEN NEXT.

 SCHIANO ADVISED INS USING THREE KEY POINTS FOR HEARING

NEXT:

 ONE, CONCERNING CHILD CUSTODY CASE OF KYOKO COX, SON

OF ANTHONY DAVID COX AND YOKO ONO BY PREVIOUS MARRIAGE.

LENNONS CLAIM NATURAL FATHER ABDUCTED SON SHORTLY AFTER

COURT IN HOUSTON, TEXAS, AWARDED LENNONS CUSTODY WITH REQUIREMENTS

CHILD BE RAISED IN US. INS BELIEVES LENNONS AND COX MAY BE

END PAGE ONE

REC-33 100-469910-12

EX-116

22 MAY 23 1972

ALL INFORMATION CONTAINED
HEREIN IS UNCLASSIFIED
DATE 2/12/82

5 MAY 25 1972

41

OPTIONAL FORM NO. 10
MAY 1962 EDITION
GSA FPMR (41 CFR) 101-11.6

UNITED STATES GOVERNMENT

Memorandum

TO : SAC, New York (100-157178)

FROM : SA ████████████████████

b7c

SUBJECT: Jerry Clyde Rubin, AKA
SM-YIP (EXTREMIST)
(Key Activist)

The subject appeared with John Lennon and
Yoko Ono at a press conference taped and shown
in WABC-TV "Eyewitness News" at 6:00pm on 1/11/72.
The press conference was held in NYC and only
Lennon was interviewed.

Rubin appeared to have his hair cut much
shorter than previously shown in other photographs.

ALL EXTREMISTS SHOULD BE
CONSIDERED DANGEROUS.

CLASS. & EXT. BY
REASON-FCIM 1-2.4.2 (2)
DATE OF REVIEW

100-157178

1703

SEARCHED ____ INDEXED ____
SERIALIZED ____ FILED ____
FBI — NEW YORK

b7c

(1-100-157178 (47)

DECLASSIFIED ON 5-3-83
BY 1678 RFP/Ebm

226

spiracies. His activities were precisely the kind protected by the First Amendment (which is not limited to citizens).

The FBI closed its file on Lennon shortly after Nixon was reelected in November 1972. Lennon spent the next year fighting the deportation order. Of course after Watergate in 1973, Nixon left the White House and Lennon stayed in the USA.

The Lennon FBI files portray a man who was a dreamer but also a fighter. They did not show his other sides: he was a working-class wit and a proud father. In an age of cynical superstars, he struggled against becoming a commodity. He worked to tell the truth not only about his wish for peace and love but also about his anger and misery.

The battle between Nixon and Lennon documented in the FBI file was an immensely significant one. "Your way of life," Lennon once said, "is a political statement." Politically, he was important because, along with Yoko, he made himself part of the movements seeking an end to the Vietnam War, for freedom, and equality for blacks and women. Together they shared the movements' hopes, arguments, confusions and occasional triumphs. They joined in.

But the battle between Nixon and Lennon documented in the FBI files should not be regarded as the central fact of Lennon's life and work. Nothing in Lennon's life was ever definitive. He was a person who was always in the process of becoming. "I know you," he sang; "you know me." We knew him in a lot of ways the FBI didn't: We knew him as an artist, and we also knew something about him as a person. The best of his work as an artist coincided with the biggest risks he took as a person. The FBI files only hint at the project that made him so significant to people who grew up in the sixties: to make the personal and the political come together.

Jon Wiener, a historian and investigative journalist, is the author of two books about John Lennon: *Come Together: John Lennon in His Time* is a social biography; *Gimme Some Truth: The John Lennon FBI Files* documents Lennon's political activism and the Nixon administration–ordered surveillance and deportation attempt in response.

MARY WILSON

THE SUPREMES WERE TO APPEAR ON THE ED SULLIVAN SHOW IN 1965. "NOTHING BUT HEARTACHES" HAD JUST BEEN RELEASED IN JUNE AND WAS OUR NEW SINGLE. WE ARRIVED IN NEW YORK CITY TO BEGIN OUR WEEK-LONG rehearsals for the show. That week was also the time that the Beatles were to appear at Shea Stadium in the Big Apple. The idea to have the Supremes meet the Beatles was brought up to us and we were delighted.

The Beatles were staying very near the Sullivan Theater at the Warwick Hotel in Manhattan, so it was arranged for the three of us to go to their hotel in between our rehearsals during the week.

The Shea Stadium gig was a sold-out biggie for the Fab Four here in the USA; America had gone crazy for them. The TV news everywhere was running clips of screaming girls surrounding the hotel where they were staying, so there was no way that the Beatles could come out to meet anyone. Also, we did not know then that they had been playing host to all of the American celebrities in town, from Bob Dylan on down the line.

The day finally came—we were to meet these wild new rock stars, so Florence, Diane and I brought our finest outfits to rehearsal to change into. When our limousine pulled up in front of the Warwick Hotel, we could hardly see out of the window for all of the screaming young faces surrounding the limo. The bodyguards went crazy trying to hold girls back, but they did not have to worry because as soon as the girls saw that we were not the Fab Four, they ran off to check out another car. It was kind of funny to see the disappointment on their faces, but also embarrassing when they did not care that we were the Supremes. They just wanted to see the Beatles.

We were very excited when we were met and escorted up to their suite, but that all changed in a matter of minutes. We had expected a beautiful large suite, with flashbulbs popping, and the guys all jumping up to shake our hands; but there was no fanfare, no celebration. Instead we could barely see anyone. It was broad daylight, but the room was quite dark. There were figures sitting around the perimeter of the room, and there we stood, all dressed up in our fur coats and gloves. We were very uncomfortable. The guys tried to make small conversation about Motown music. Paul was very friendly, and Ringo cracked a few jokes. George as I recall seemed very shy. John was very quiet; I recall him only saying hello and asking about Motown musicians. We asked our publicist to get us out of there. Years later, George told me that they too wanted us to leave. I guess we were too prim and proper. George said that they thought we would be hip, being black and all.

George, Ringo and I became fairly good friends while I was touring in the U.K. in the 1970s. My then husband, Pedro, and I hung out a lot with Ringo in Monte Carlo, and we would visit George and his wife at their beautiful English castle. While shooting pool at George's home, Pedro saw a stretch limousine sitting out in the garage on blocks. The car used to be John's, and George had come to own it. Pedro cut a deal for something like thirty pounds.

We eventually had the limo shipped back to the States. While we drove it for years, unfortunately, the stretch never worked properly, always overheating. Eventually, I had Sotheby's auction it off. The value of the car because of all the stars who had owned it was enormous. A gentleman in Finland was the highest bidder; he wanted it, he said, because it had belonged to John Lennon.

Mary Wilson is a founding member of legendary vocal group the Supremes. Scoring twelve number-one hits in five years, the Supremes were unquestionably the most popular female group of the 1960s and were inducted into the Rock and Roll Hall of Fame in 1988.

London Calling   BARBARA WORTON

I WAS FOURTEEN IN 1963, IN MY FRESHMAN YEAR IN HIGH
SCHOOL. I WAS IN SCHOOL JUST ONE WEEK WHEN MY BOY-
FRIEND FROM SECOND GRADE DUMPED ME.

IT WAS A SHOCK. BUT, ABOUT A WEEK LATER, I WAS OVER
it because this new kid came to school. Black hair, blue eyes, really
adorable and straight out of immigration from England. So, he has
this great accent, and he's sitting right in front of me in homeroom.
Alphabetical order, and I was in love. We started hanging out, and he
introduced me to the Beatles months before anyone else even knew
there was a place called Liverpool. After school, we'd go back to his
house and listen to music. And I liked this guy from England, but I
loved the Beatles.

I was one of the first members of their U.S. fan club and adored
John Lennon with every inch of my being. He was a poet; I was, too.
I loved his voice, his evil sense of humor, and he absolutely had the
best hair. But nobody really knew that I loved John Lennon. That was
a secret, a really big secret. John was so cute and smart. People would
just laugh at me if they knew I thought I was good enough for John.

But, finally the Beatles made it to the *Ed Sullivan Show,* and all
the kids who had been laughing at me in school were instant Beatle-

maniacs. My English boyfriend was now hot, hot, hot. Women were throwing themselves at him, and I got dumped again.

One postdumping Saturday night, I was home baby-sitting and feeling sorry for myself—singing into my hairbrush—"Yesterday, all my troubles seemed so far away"—and crying and slumping around. And the phone rang, and a voice, very official-sounding, said, "We have a transatlantic call from London, England, for Barbara. Is she available?"

I said, yes. And this woman on the other end of the line said, "Hello. Is this Barbara?"

I answered, "Yes, it is."

"Well, hello, darling, this is Cynthia Lennon."

My heart stopped.

"I'm just calling you because you were one of the first members of the Beatles fan club in the U.S., and, well, John and the boys just thought it would be really nice if we picked up the phone and called all the people who helped to make them so hugely popular in the States and just let them know just how much we appreciate the support. And on behalf of my husband, John, I'd like to say thank you. Ta-da."

Thank you, too, I said, and hung up.

Now, back in 1963, stuff like this happened, Murray the K, Cousin Brucie, the WMCA Good Guys, they did stuff like this. And even though I knew this call couldn't be real, I really wanted it to be.

Monday, I showed up at school, and I walked into English class. One of my friends was talking to the teacher, whispering, and they were looking at me. I sat down, and the teacher said, looking straight at me, "I hear someone in the class is getting transatlantic phone calls from London."

My heart started pounding, and I just sat there and sort of looked down. Then he said, "Barbara, it's you, right? You got a call from Cynthia Lennon?" And I looked up at him with deep loathing, and I didn't say anything, but my friend and some of the other kids were looking at me with stupid grins.

Then he said, "John Lennon is your favorite Beatle, right?" And I answered, flatly, "Yes. May I be excused?" I ran out of that classroom and into the girls' room right across the hall. I stayed there until after the bell rang. I heard somebody open the girls' room door and call Barbara, but I didn't answer.

The next day, I came back to school and nobody remembered what had happened to me in English class. I think "She Loves You" was released that morning. So my humiliation was no longer news.

A year later, the Beatles were our lives, my life, for sure. I went to see them live on the *Ed Sullivan Show*, sat about two feet from John in the second or third row of the balcony. Saw them at Shea Stadium twice. I don't remember how many times I saw *A Hard Day's Night* and *Help!* and *Yellow Submarine*. But I hung on every one of John's lines. He said the things I always wanted to say. He was funny, and he became my voice, my hero.

The last time I saw John was in the late 1970s. It was the height of the designer jeans era, and I was walking up Fifth Avenue right past Rockefeller Center, and he was walking toward me. I saw him and thought, oh, there's someone I knew in high school. Then I realized it was John, and I can't imagine what kind of look I had on my face, but I must have terrified him because I saw his whole facial expression change. But he kept walking toward me—brave man—and then, we were side by side, and I thought I heard him say, "Nice pants." We were both wearing Paris 2000 jeans. I didn't say anything back, but I just felt for two seconds, you know, if John had met me, if we did know each other, we probably would have been friends.

Barbara Worton is a writer, actress and communications executive.

RITCHIE YORKE

WHILE THE UNITED STATES AND BRITAIN HAVE THEIR OWN PARTICULAR LINKS WITH THE LIFE OF JOHN ONO LENNON, CANADIANS ALSO HAVE A VERY SPECIAL AND INDIVIDUAL IMPRESSION OF JOHN.

For a time there during the 1969 Summer of Love, Canada became almost a second home for the Lennons as they pursued their various media-driven initiatives in an effort to bring peace and harmony to an ugly, violent world.

While it is factually true that the U.S. government declined to extend John Lennon the courtesy of a visitor's visa throughout 1969, one feels it is necessary to point out that regardless of immigration restriction, things were always different in Canada. Canada as a nation was simply far more welcoming and encouraging of the Lennons in their peace activities.

Canada had not taken part in the military campaign in Vietnam or Cambodia, just as it declined to be part of the recent invasion of Iraq by U.S. forces lacking U.N. approval. Canada's proximity to the American industrial-military machine may well account for the country's unwillingness to join in these aggressive actions. It might even be said that as the nearest neighbour of the United States,

Canadians understand the American military mind-set more acutely than most.

The Lennons' first visit to Canada in 1969 (John of course had previously touched down in Canada as part of a Beatles tour some years earlier) was almost an accident, if one believes in such things. Whatever it was that drove their desires, they lobbed into Toronto International Airport in May, fresh from an ill-fated stopover in the Bahamas. It was only a couple of months after their hitherto secret marriage in Gibraltar and the resulting Amsterdam bed-in for peace. Amsterdam had been chosen by John and Yoko because it was "quiet, friendly and British."

When the time came to organise a second bed-in—and one that was strategically located as close to U.S. territory as possible—the couple opted for the Bahamas, also a country with British colonial origins.

Supposedly tourist-friendly Bahamas people somehow missed the point, and after the Lennons were charged $130 for a room-service orange juice, press officer Derek Taylor pulled the pin and the party flew to Toronto looking for a new bed-in location. I'll never forget that cryptic call from Taylor, a relatively close friend over some years of interacting in our chosen professions. I was at my desk at the *Toronto Globe and Mail*, mulling over some album review or another, when Derek came on the line inquiring if I could slip down to the nearby King Edward Hotel for a parlay with John and Yoko, who'd just arrived in town.

I ended up escaping from a corridor full of screaming Beatles fans as we beat a hasty retreat to the hotel's basement in order for the three of them (John, Yoko and Derek Taylor) to be transported by limousine to the airport for the flight to Montreal. After a series of urgent phone calls, Derek Taylor had figured out that Montreal's Queen Elizabeth Hotel seemed to be the ideal venue for the second bed-in.

And it was. After a weeklong odyssey of meeting the media (and hosting such enlightened dignitaries as Dr. Timothy Leary, jazz writer Nat Hentoff and the Smothers brothers Tom and Dick) and recording an impromptu "Give Peace a Chance"—ultimately set to become a universal peace anthem, in addition to being John's first release without the other Beatles—the Montreal bed-in could be considered a profound success. A couple of days after they'd departed Toronto, I managed to persuade my editors to let me head down to Montreal to chronicle some of the historic bed-in events unfolding there.

I remember writing at the time that peace had been very much to the fore in the Lennon suite—assorted John doodlings, peace mottos and phrases were randomly attached to the walls. Everywhere there were pink and white flowers which had been hastily organised by Capitol/EMI Records and other well-wishers.

There were no security guards in evidence, only the Beatles' lean and unmuscled press officer Derek Taylor. Derek was unlikely to be able to deter any potential physical aggression toward his charges, but he could do wonders

Out in the December snow surrounding the Mississauga estate of singer Ronnie Hawkins, who hosted the Lennons on their historic Canadian visit in December 1969. Left to right: Author and journalist Ritchie Yorke with John and Yoko and U.S. human rights campaigner and comedian Dick Gregory.

with words. And he was fast on his feet. I doubt if anybody could have served John and Yoko better than dear Derek, who died in 1997 at the age of a very young sixty-five.

And whereas John and Yoko might have comfortably lounged around in holiday mode on palatial country estates, as other Beatles were doing, the Lennons had this extraordinary urge and need to put something back. To stand up for reason in an unreasonable world, to take advantage of their extraordinary media profile to refocus public attitude and outlook on the murdering of other humans.

Even now, only an ignoramus would question their motives. It's something that I've often reflected upon over the years, and in particular those difficult days that followed December 8, 1980.

Throughout the Montreal bed-in there had been informal background discussions within the camp about the possibility of arranging a meeting between the Lennons and the Canadian prime minister, Pierre Elliott Trudeau. It was something that we all aspired toward and its appropriate time and place was not far distant on the road ahead.

The next Canadian occasion for the Lennons would be their unexpected involvement in the Toronto Rock 'n' Roll Revival in September. A group of eager Canadians, including myself, had managed to convince John and Yoko to take part in an outdoor concert which featured the Doors, Little Richard, Chuck Berry, Jerry Lee Lewis, Bo Diddley, Gene Vincent, Alice Cooper, Junior Walker and the All-Stars and others.

The event would mark John's first live performance outside the Beatles since the Liverpool quartet's journey. It would teach him a valuable lesson: that he didn't necessarily require Paul, George or Ringo to put on a heck of a show. On this occasion, he'd formed the Plastic Ono Band with Eric Clapton, Klaus Voormann and Alan White.

But it was the Lennons' third Canadian sojourn for 1969 that would most intrigue my long-term memory cells. Each of the Lennon journeys to Canada was of a pioneering nature—each time we would follow them out upon the untrodden snow of some metaphorical snowstorm, leaving a single line of fresh footprints where we'd traveled.

And of all these highly significant events, the memory that clings most clearly to me is of John's acute nervousness at the prospect of meeting Prime Minister Pierre Trudeau. I'd witnessed John and Yoko work their way through an assortment of different dilemmas and situations during the course of the War Is Over If You Want It peace campaign. But there'd never been anything quite like this frozen morning in the Canadian capital of Ottawa as John and Yoko prepared for their first interaction with a world leader.

I'd never seen John in the grip of such intense and restless nervous energy. I can see and feel those images now, lips pursed almost grimly with granny glasses perched at the end of his nose, nervously pacing the bone-colored carpet of his Ottawa hotel room, fiddling with the black taffeta tie which defined the cut of his black Pierre Cardin suit. I can even smell the pungent fumes of Continental tobacco as John lit one Gitane (a robust brand of French cigarette) after another. His concern was contagious: some rays of it touched each of us playing at being cool in his room that morning.

Looking back, one presumes that the extent of John's concern centred around the pending interaction with a politician of any persuasion. It was a direct connection into the web of the often-despised Establishment. Less than a month earlier, John had snubbed his nose at that power centre by returning his MBE medal to the Queen.

But Pierre Elliott Trudeau, as John was about to discover, was cut from a wholly different cloth. He was significantly more than just a frontline politician of the late 1960s. And much more than the mere leader of small liberal Canada (ironically he was the head of the appropriately named Liberal Party in Canada which lived up to its name). He was a fifty-year-old philosopher and widely traveled student with an intense curiosity. He didn't govern by polls: he acted by the alliance of reason and relevance. An unlikely purveyor of political persuasion as it was cultivated in this era. In my sixty-odd years, I have never encountered a politician of the calibre or class of Pierre Elliott Trudeau.

Pierre Trudeau was decidedly different than the norm. His progress was not in any way connected with the prevailing political agenda dominating this era. To his eternal credit, Mr. Trudeau had not hesitated to declare the degree of difference from his less-enlightened contemporaries. In a notable May 26, 1978, speech to the United Nations General Assembly Special Session on Disarmament he declared:

The principles of laissez-faire were undoubtedly instrumental in bringing about the extraordinary growth in wealth which accompanied the Industrial Revolution. But the Industrial Revolution, it will be recalled, was hardly a tale of equality and fraternity. In terms of misery, disease, injustice, wanton indignity and sheer wastage of human lives, it easily surpassed the years of the Terror. Indeed, if a tally could be made in the four quarters of the globe, one wonders if it would not be a match for the tens of millions sacrificed by Stalin in the name of the dictatorship of the proletariat, when he attempted to force the backward Soviet society through its own industrial revolution.

These were certainly not the utterings—spoken or unspoken—of your common, everyday politician circa 1969.

And nor was Mr. Trudeau's perceptive comment from 1984: "Nuclear weapons exist. They probably always will. And they work, with horrible efficiency. They threaten the very future of our species. We have no choice but to manage that risk. Never again can we put the task out of our minds; not trivialise it; nor make it routine. Nor dare we lose heart."

There wasn't any doubt that these were powerful and profound comments at a time when politicians liked to plot from within a vacuum of honesty and their outright deception about the highly debatable values of the nuclear weapons that threatened to obliterate our very existence.

Pierre Trudeau was not admired by the right-wing custodians of other countries in 1969, as the Vietnam fiasco continued to simmer in the public consciousness thanks to the uncensored coverage of that awful conflagration. The terrible truths were invading millions of U.S. households at every news break. The public may not have been sufficiently equipped to process that sort of information.

Disgraced U.S. President Richard Nixon reportedly detested Mr. Trudeau, which is hardly surprising. In fact, when the contents of the Watergate tapes were transcribed, it emerged that Tricky Dickie had described the Canadian leader as "that asshole Trudeau" due to differences over U.S. policy in Vietnam. Mr. Trudeau's immediate response to that blatant insult was simplistic and righteous. "I've been called worse things by better people," he shrugged, right on the money.

The intellectually deprived Ronald Reagan, after the first G-7 summit in 1981 at Montebello, Quebec, dismissed Trudeau's "woolly-minded, impractical liberal thinking."

In his memoirs, Reagan revealingly commented on an argument which Mr. Trudeau had initiated at the G-7 conference with that other right-wing demagogue, U.K. Prime Minister Margaret Thatcher. "Pierre bitterly lit into Margaret, the chairman of the meeting, and told her she was being heavy-handed and undemocratic. I was horrified by his rudeness and the insulting way that he spoke to her," noted Reagan's ghost-writer. Gee whiz!

In the interests of fairness, we should point out that Mr. Trudeau reflected rather magnanimously in his memoirs that "Reagan was not a man for thoughtful policy discussions, but he was pleasant and congenial, and my children found him entertaining." Ouch!

Trudeau's aides were privately less reserved in their expressed off-the-record contempt for Reagan's basic dumbness and his inability to answer random press conference questions without prewritten prepared answers.

So Lennon's meeting with Trudeau was always going to be much more than just another publicist-staged politician-meets-pop-star-for-mutual-benefit routine.

Other political leaders had predictably declined the prospect of a meeting with the Beatles' most outspoken and therefore controversial member. Queen Elizabeth was apparently miffed over the MBE incident. British Labor Prime Minister Harold Wilson simply didn't want to know him at all. Newly elected U.S. President Richard Nixon was equally appalled at the prospect of any association with, God forbid, a convicted hash smoker and rabble-rouser and possible unifier of the rapidly expanding antiwar movement, which had attracted millions of concerned young people around North America. Nixon viewed John Lennon as a huge threat to keeping the lid on counterculture objections to the Vietnam War.

What it all came down to was fairly elementary. When our initial efforts to link up Messrs. Lennon and Trudeau through the auspices of the Canadian prime minister's office were not automatically dismissed or sneered at, we knew that we were in with a real chance. This is what was called a live lead.

One of the provisos that the PM's office insisted on, right from the first snatches of encouragement, was that there couldn't be any advance publicity of any kind. No hints, no cleverly baited indicators, nothing at all.

The PM's office clearly didn't want to create a circus. And neither did we. And they astutely realised early on how easily this planned scenario could deteriorate into an unmanageable farce. The Lennon camp didn't want that situation to happen, either.

So despite a burning desire to tell the world about this unexpected development, mum was the word. Our lips were clamped shut.

And so on a bitterly cold but brilliantly sunny Tuesday morning at 10:30 in the final days of the 1960s—December 21, 1969—we found ourselves clustered in John and Yoko's Ottawa hotel room attempting to calm John's nerves. Trying to make him feel a little more au fait about the forthcoming meeting with the prime minister.

Yoko, quite naturally, was doing all she could to comfort John and ease his attack of nerves. But John was pretty seriously enmeshed in his nervousness. I still find myself silently pondering why this extraordinary individual, this man of so many parts—who'd long since met most of rock 'n' roll's royalty—was in such a nervous state at the thought of fronting up to have a chat with Pierre Trudeau.

I couldn't help but wonder about the logic behind it all. After you've met Elvis Presley, Ed Sullivan and a thousand or more aspirants to his music cultural throne, why would you be freaked at the opportunity of meeting a prime minister?

Later I would realise that any world leader would be likely to intimidate a member of the showbiz fraternity, especially if that leader spoke openly and didn't beat around the bush. The circumstances surrounding a meeting with any prime minister, let alone Pierre Trudeau, would undoubtedly intimidate even as imposing a Hollywood superstar as actor Marlon Brando. In 1978 Brando attended a meeting with Prime Minister Trudeau to try and obtain some government funding for a film about native people. To support his case, the renowned actor explained that he felt that Canada and the United States had a common native tradition. Whereupon Mr. Trudeau noted, a trifle acidly, "Ah, there are differences in the way we treated our native people. You hunted them down and murdered them. We starved them to death."

After the meeting, the venerable actor admitted to the PM's communications director: "That's the most frightened I've ever been in my life. He's [Trudeau's] the most intimidating person I've ever met."

We certainly weren't expecting our get-together with Mr. Trudeau to be anything but amiable. And we'd tried to make that abundantly clear to John. From a considered distance, Mr. Trudeau appeared to have an understanding and empathy toward the youth culture of which John and Yoko were reluctant figureheads, if not leaders. We'd tried to apprise the Lennons of the prime minister's diverse background and intellectual track record as we zoomed across a frozen Canadian countryside in the private CN Rail observation car which we'd hired for the journey.

The first stage of the journey took us from Toronto to Montreal where our private car was shunted into a platform of the Gare Centrale. After a late afternoon press conference at the Queen Elizabeth Hotel, where John had recorded "Give Peace a Chance" during the Montreal bed-in a mere six months ago, we returned to the privacy of our carriage for a meeting with representatives of the Le Dain Drug Commission. It would be a most enthralling evening parked in the bowels of Montreal's main railway station.

Early next day, our carriage was attached to the Ottawa morning rail service and we pulled into the frozen city to be greeted by a temperature of minus 12 C. We were picked up in limousines and transported to a hotel where John and Yoko prepared themselves for the upcoming meeting. And John proceeded to struggle with his attack of the nerves.

At precisely 10:30 AM, the media was notified that John and Yoko would be visiting with the Canadian prime minister that morning. Twenty-five minutes later, they pulled up at the East Block of Parliament House in a limousine driven by the man who would subsequently become Canada's ambassador to the United Nations, Alan Rock. The meeting was intended to run for fifteen minutes but ended up expanding onward to fill a total of fifty-one minutes before the world's most newsworthy couple emerged from Mr. Trudeau's inner sanctum. One immediately noticed that John was looking extremely relieved.

There had been many points of fruitful discussion and numerous opportunities for John and Yoko to outline their philosophy on peace. Prime Minister Trudeau was most encouraging of the Lennons' antiwar aspirations. He complimented them on the War Is Over campaign and he indicated official support for the Peace

Festival event which John and Yoko had unveiled a few days earlier at the largest press conference ever held in Toronto. And Mr. Trudeau encouraged the Lennons to continue their campaign of standing up for peace.

John was equally enthusiastic about the Canadian leader's open-mindedness. "If there were more leaders like Mister Trudeau," John bleated into a battery of microphones and camera lenses, "the world would have peace. You people in Canada don't realise how lucky you are."

Added Yoko, in her soft Japanese-accented voice: "We're just enthralled meeting Mister Trudeau—he is a beautiful person. It gives us great incentive seeing people like him in the establishment."

Later John told me that Mr. Trudeau had talked about how important it was for him to keep in close contact with young people at large. He emphasised that he would like to meet with the Lennons in less formal circumstances for further discussions.

Mr. Trudeau and the Lennons had found much of mutual interest in their wide-ranging discussion.

Later John would comment, "The political climate in Canada is completely different from any other country. The politicians here at least want to hear what young people think. They'll talk, and that is the important first step."

Pointing out that their conversation had been mainly concerned with generalisations, John noted that "we achieved something like communication. . . . Talk is the state of any communication."

Not surprisingly, some of the crustier members of the local media were a tad less than overwhelmed by the Lennon War Is Over crusade. U.K. media, in particular the tabloid press, had earlier railed against the Lennons' perceived naïveté. And even in Canada, and despite the official nod the prime ministerial meeting had given the Lennon peace efforts, there would be the odd grumpy editorial and random discontent in editorials such as this excerpt from the *Medicine Hat News,* Christmas Eve, 1969: "Most Canadians cannot help but react with scepticism to Lennon's current crusade. His goal of world peace is an admirable one, of course, but his methods of realising this ideal are naïve. An end to war between nations—to official violence—cannot be achieved by buying full page ads in the *New York Times* or by bleating 'Give Peace a Chance' in the streets of Toronto. These are exercises in futility. Theatrics that don't resolve anything.

Every sane person on Earth wants peace, but most of us are sophisticated enough to know that only our leaders can end war."

The *Medicine Hat* piece also called into question Lennon's motivation in taking part in the peace initiative. "These rumors (of Lennon as a latent politician wooing tomorrow's electorate) have persisted because Lennon has been the most politically conscious of the four Beatles. He has deliberately identified himself with the Now Generation—in fact he helped mould it—and often speaks his mind on such gut issues as pot, peace and pollution. And developing an authoritative image, it must be remembered, is a prerequisite for any aspiring politician. When seen in this context, therefore, Lennon's Canadian peace offensive gradually becomes less an exercise in wayward idealism and more a shrewd attempt to manufacture credentials."

Goodness gracious.

Of course not all Canadians would be so offensively judgmental. In a Toronto conversation with communications prophet the late Marshall McLuhan, which had been filmed by U.S. CBS TV for use in the final *60 Minutes* show of the 1960s, there would be no shortage of revelations.

"The Beatles' pattern is one that has to be scrapped," John informed McLuhan, prefacing the inevitable breakup of his old band, for anybody interested. "If it remains the same, it's a monument, or a museum, and one thing this is about is no museums. . . . The Beatles turned into a museum, so they have to be scrapped or deformed or changed."

John also alerted McLuhan to the British variations on the American concept of the star system. "We're not like the Americans to be hyped by Hollywood. The attitude is to be quiet, do a dance at the London Palladium, and stop talking about peace. That's what we get in London."

According to McLuhan, it was all about adrenaline. "This is why dinosaurs ended in sudden death, because as the environment became more and more hostile, more and more adrenaline was released into their bodies and they got bigger and bigger and then collapsed.

"It could happen to America," McLuhan continued. "It already happened to the British Empire. Adrenaline just gave out. In fact, your [Beatles] songs represented the end of that big adrenaline flow. As far as the U.K. was concerned, Beatles music was the end of the adrenaline. And the beginning of peace and contentment."

But the great Toronto-based visionary had not foreseen the British involvement in the invasion of Iraq.

Following the historic meeting with the prime minister, the Lennons returned to Ronnie Hawkins' suburban home in Mississauga, just outside Toronto, to wrap up their Canadian trip. As we boarded the flight at Ottawa Airport, a rather relieved John joked about the extent of his nervousness a few hours earlier. It was funny now, but it hadn't been all that amusing a few hours ago.

Sharing our flight from Ottawa back to Toronto was former Canadian prime minister Lester Pearson. It was notably ironic that the man regarded as the father of Canadian peacekeeping—and the winner of the Nobel Peace Prize in 1957—would be on the same Air Canada flight as the Lennons. We politely asked the cabin steward to pass along John and Yoko's greetings, which were warmly received. It was a serendipitous conclusion to what had turned out to be a wonderful first encounter between a political leader and an integral figure from the youth culture.

The next day, Christmas Eve, the Lennons set forth in Ronnie Hawkins' white Rolls Royce through a volley of snow flurries to what is now known as Lester B. Pearson International Airport for the flight home. After returning to London and reflecting on his weeklong trip to Canada, John observed with obvious conviction: "It was the best trip we've ever had. We got more done for peace this week than in our whole lives."

That was a huge and revealing statement. And I do think John meant it.

Ritchie Yorke is a respected author, music journalist, producer and historian. He is widely regarded as an elder statesman of Australian rock journalism.

Paper Cups   YOKO ONO LENNON

In 1968, John and I decided to go to the opening of the Arts Lab, a gathering place for students and cutting edge artists in London. They asked me to display one of my sculptures there for this special occasion for them. So John and I wanted to see how it was displayed. We were full of expectation. We wore something nice, but not too grand, and got in the car. We were supposed to give a ride to Paul and Ringo who happened to want a ride into town.

So the car picked up Paul, and then Ringo. As the car neared the Arts Lab John said, "You know, Yoko's sculpture is being shown. You want to come? You're welcome." Paul just said he couldn't. Ringo said "I'm sorry, John, but I can't," So we got off without them. When we opened the door to the Arts Lab, everybody looked at us. That was normal. But then, to our dismay, they all turned their backs, quickly, almost in unison, and started to resume chatting with each other!

At the time, we were both very popular people. John, of course, was a Beatle. I was the "high priestess of the avant-garde," as the critics had hailed me. So it surprised us a little that this hip art crowd would turn their backs to us like that. My sculpture was in a very visible spot. But people just ignored "it" and "us" and kept talking.

John was not fazed. He made sprightly steps to the counter and asked for two coffees. "Two coffees, please. For Yoko and me." The girl took one look at John with angry eyes and said "you get your own coffee." John went to the machine, and got two coffees in paper cups, and led me to the staircase. We sat in the middle of the narrow staircase going up, and looked down at the crowd.

John and I could hardly drink our coffee. People kept going up and down the narrow stairs shouting, "Excuse me, excuse me." Each time, we had to stand up and make way for them. It was intense watching what was going on in the party down there, too. Some people were about to bump into my sculpture which was placed on the floor without a stand. The work was a very special version of *Mend Piece*—a group of sculptural pieces impossible to put together—a mend piece which can't be mended. It gave me a laugh when I came up with the idea. But now it was not so funny.

"At least, they should have put a rope around it or something," I muttered. John, noticing my worry, took my hand and said, "You know, when the going is rough, we keep our chins up. That's what we do." This was the first time it was shown to us that together, we were NOT SO POPULAR! Indeed. However, as John said in "WONSAPONATIME," "Being in love they cloong even the more together man."

Since then there were many times we had to keep our chins up. It was harder when I had to take the brunt of the attack after John's passing. But I always remembered what John had said in the Arts Lab that evening, and kept my chin up through the storms.

WONSAPONATIME

there was two Balloons called Jock and Yono. They were strictly in love-bound to happen in a million years. They were together man. Unfortunatimetable they both seemed to have previous experience— which kept calling them one way oranother (you know howitis). But they battled on against overwhelming oddities, includo some of there beast friends. Being in love they cloong even the more together man—but some of the poisonessmonster of outrated buslodedshithrowers did stick slightly and they occasionally had to resort to the drycleaners. Luckily this did not kill them and they werent banned from the olympic games. They lived hopefully ever after, and who could blame them. j.o.l.

ACKNOWLEDGMENTS

Many creative people played a role in making *Memories of John Lennon* possible. Thank you to Jeanne Welsh, Lisa Iannucci, Kristin Levine, Elizabeth Circo and the staff of Adler Robin Books, Dana Beck and the staff of Bill Adler Books, and Peter Shukat and Jonas Herbsman of Shukat, Arrow, Hafer & Weber, LLP. Also, many thanks to Elliot Mintz, Bob Gruen, Peter Brown, Karon Crosby, and Ritchie Yorke.

This book would not have been possible without the remarkable work of Willa Shalit.

CREDITS

10   Illustration © 2005 Joan Baez.

14   Photo by Harry Benson, previously published in *Once There Was a Way: Photographs of the Beatles* by Harry Benson (New York: Harry Abrams, 2003).

17   Chuck Berry selection, By the editors, from *The Ballad of John and Yoko,* © Rolling Stone Press, 1982.

18   Jello Biafra illustration © Jello Biafra and excerpt courtesy of *Alternative Tentacles.*

27   Illustration © Bono.

34   Photograph courtesy of Mike Cadwallader.

37   Ray Charles selection, By the editors, from *The Ballad of John and Yoko,* © Rolling Stone Press, 1982.

43   "War Is Over" photograph © Yoko Ono. Reprinted with permission.

55   Julie Gold excerpt courtesy of *Performing Songwriter Magazine.*

60   "Season of Glass" by Yoko Ono © 1981. Reprinted with permission.

61   Bed-in photograph by Ivor Sharp, courtesy of Yoko Ono. Reprinted with permission.

67, 69   Photographs © Harry Goodwin. All rights reserved. Reprinted with permission.

CREDITS

CREDITS

ABOUT THE EDITOR

Yoko Ono Lennon's family emigrated from Japan after World War II and settled in New York, where Yoko, who had studied philosophy and music, worked as a conceptual artist in the early 1960s. In 1966 she met John Lennon. She was married to John from 1969 until his death in 1980. Together they collaborated on revolutionary art, film and music projects and spent much of their time on peace and humanitarian efforts. Since John's death, Yoko has released her own records, classified as experimental compositions and avant-garde rock and roll. She is a multimedia artist and currently resides in New York City.